Concepts

of Depression

APPROACHES TO BEHAVIOR PATHOLOGY SERIES

Brendan Maher — Series Editor

CONCEPTS OF DEPRESSION

Joseph Mendels

John Wiley & Sons, Inc.

New York • London • Sydney • Toronto

Library of Congress Catalog Card Number: 70-120707

ISBN 0-471-59350-8 Cloth
ISBN 0-471-59351-6 Paper

Printed in the United States of America

10 9 8 7 6 5 4 3 2 1

To Ora

SERIES PREFACE

Abnormal psychology may be studied in many different ways. One traditional method of approach emphasizes the description of clinical syndromes with an extensive use of case histories to illustrate the central phenomena and the psychological processes believed to underlie them. Another common position is found in the adoption of a systematic theory (such as psychodynamic or behavioral) as a framework within which important problems of abnormal psychology may be delineated and interpreted.

Whether systematic or eclectic, descriptive or interpretive, the teaching of a course in abnormal psychology faces certain difficult problems. Just as in other areas of science, abnormal psychology has exhibited a rapid increase in knowledge and in the rate at which new knowledge is being acquired. It is becoming more and more difficult for the college teacher to keep abreast of contemporary developments over as wide a range of subjects as abnormal psychology encompasses. Even in the areas of his personal interest and special competence the instructor may be hard pressed to cover significant concepts and findings with real comprehensiveness.

Adding to this spate of new knowledge is the fact that, in the field of abnormal psychology, we are witnessing a resurgence of enthusiasm for empirical research of an experimental kind together with a growth of interest in deviant behavior on the part of other scientists, notably the geneticists, neurobiologists, biochemists on the one hand and epidemiologists, anthropologists and social scientists on the other. It is less and less possible to claim mastery of a topic area in abnormal psychology when approaching it purely from the standpoint of a single psychological theory. An adequate understanding of any central topic now depends on familiarity with literature coming from many quarters of the scientific community.

Knowledge multiplies but time does not. Working within the limits of forty to fifty lecture hours available for the usual course in general abnormal psychology, it has become necessary for the student to turn more and more often to specialized outside reading to acquire the depth that cannot be given by any one textbook or by any one instructor. Although much can be gained by reading a range of selected reprints, these are often written originally for audiences other than the undergraduates and for purposes too narrowly technical to be entirely suited to instruction.

The present volume is one of a series developed to meet the need for depth of coverage in the central topic areas of abnormal psychology. The series is prepared with certain criteria in mind. Each volume has been planned to be scientifically authoritative, to be written with the clarity and directness necessary for the introductory student, but with a sophistication and timeliness of treatment that should render it of value to the advanced student and the fellow-specialist. Selection of the topics to be included in the series has been guided by a decision to concentrate on problem areas that are systematically and empirically important: in each case there are significant theoretical problems to be examined and a body of research literature to cast light on the several solutions that are adduced. Although it is anticipated that the student may read one or more of these volumes in addition to a standard text, the total series will cover the major part of a typical course in abnormal psychology and could well be used in place of a single text.

We are in a period of exciting growth and change in abnormal psychology. Concepts and hypotheses that have dominated the field for over half a century are giving place to new and provocative viewpoints. Much of this has been accomplished in one short decade: it is clear that the character of the field will be changed even more radically in the decades to come. It is the hope of the editor and the contributors to this series that they will play a useful part in preparing the coming generation of psychopathologists for the challenge of the years that lie ahead.

BRENDAN MAHER

PREFACE

We live in the looming shadow of the Bomb. We live in war. We live against a background of poverty and deprivation, on which is imposed unprecedented wealth and the ambiguous values of advanced technology. We live in the midst of injustice and corruption, decadence and anguish made available by modern communications for us all tu see. And men race to the moon while the techniques of chemical warfare are perfected.

We are continually forced to confront the questions of individual responsibility and individual commitment in a society whose standards contradict its own premises.

We do not know ourselves or those we love or those who live around us, because ultimately each of us is alone. But we know enough to need to understand more, and the imperfection of human communication is a barrier to be struggled against each day.

There is no rational mind, facing these issues, that is not depressed. The contradictions and choices are real, they affect each one of us, and the sane, rational response is depression.

But most of us do not become clinically depressed. Neither the dangers and horrors that are part of contemporary society, nor the limitations of our personal situations lead most of us into that burden of hopelessness and despair that is sufficiently constant and sufficiently restrictive to normal life to constitute pathological depression.

How do so many people evade the response that seems most inevitable? It is entirely possible that we delude ourselves. The myriad threatening forces of our lives might so utterly engulf us if we faced them head on all the time that we create for ourselves a protective system of delusions—a fortification of defenses—designed to produce detachment for the purpose of promoting our own survival.

But there is something more: the manifestations of clinical depression —the sense of futility, the certainty of personal inadequacy, the fear and the immobilization at the most trivial level—are only in part produced by looking at reality and not liking it. They are often counterpointed by qualities of unreality, mistaken judgment, and unfounded fear, and are usually focused, not on the large issues of the times but on the bread-and-butter problems of daily living and on the emotional problems of communication and need.

Who among us becomes depressed? And why?

What constitutes the Achilles Heel of those who suffer this condition? An aberrant gene? A childhood loss? The method by which our parents raised us? Or the personal problems and stresses of adult life?

This book is designed to describe and examine clinical depression and to illuminate the forces that make it distinct from the contemporary dilemma.

Joseph Mendels

ACKNOWLEDGMENTS

I am indebted to the following for permission to reproduce copyright materials.

Table 2 is reproduced with the permission of Dr. C. Perris and *Acta Psychiatrica Scandinavica.*

Table 3 is reproduced with permission from "Depression: Categories, Mechanisms and Phenomena, by H. E. Lehmann," in *Pharmacotherapy of Depression.* J. O. Cole and J. R. Wittenborn (Eds.). Springfield: Thomas, 1966.

The definitions in the Appendix are reprinted with the permission of the American Psychiatric Association.

Chapter 4 is partially based on a paper "The Nosology of Depression: The Endogenous-Reactive Concept" by J. Mendels and C. Cochrane, *American Journal of Psychiatry, 124,* (May 1968, Supplement), 1–11. Chapters 7 and 8 draw on a paper "Towards a Biology of Depression: Some Suggestions from Neurophysiology" by P. Whybrow and J. Mendels. *American Journal of Psychiatry,* 1969, *125,* 4, 1491–1500. Drs. Cochrane and Whybrow and the American Psychiatric Association have kindly given permission to use this material.

The material on sleep and depression (Chapter 8) is drawn from several reports that I published with Dr. David R. Hawkins. I would like to acknowledge his cooperation and the permission to reproduce it from the publishers of the journals in which the material originally appeared: *Archives of General Psychiatry, American Journal of Psychiatry,* and *Mental Hygiene.* Miss Sandra Koch patiently typed several drafts of the manuscript.

My wife encouraged and assisted me at all stages of this manuscript. Without her it probably would never have been done.

J. M.

CONTENTS

Concepts

of Depression

CHAPTER ONE

INTRODUCTION

Depression is as old as man. It has accompanied him throughout his history, and the world's literature has chronicled it with the intensity and care that so ancient and so widespread a condition warrants. Depression is a universal experience; the emotions of sadness and grief are an intrinsic facet of the human condition. However, pathological depression—that overwhelming, often apparently unprompted despair—is distinguishable from grief by its intensity, duration, and evident irrationality and by its effects on the lives of those who suffer it.

The word "depression" is used in many ways: to describe a mood, a symptom, a syndrome (or a collection of signs and symptoms) as well as a specific group of illnesses. This multiple use of the term and the looseness of definitions can be very confusing. In this book we are concerned with depression (and mania) as a form of psychopathology (symptom, syndrome, or illness). The everyday mood disturbance that we call sadness or depression is beyond our scope here.

Depression is very common. Although exact figures are not available, it is probable that about five out of every 100 adults become significantly depressed at some time in their lives. Many of these people never seek help, and of those who do the majority can be treated without hospitalization.

Thousands of years ago the Book of Job recorded psychopathological depression.

"Wherefore then hast thou brought me forth out of the womb? Oh that I had given up the ghost and no eye had seen me!" Job cried and, later in his long agony, "I was at ease, but he hath broken me asunder . . . he poureth out my gall upon the ground . . . I have sewed sackcloth upon my skin and defiled my horn in the dust . . . My face is foul with weeping and on my eyelids is the shadow of death. . . . I have said to corruption, Thou art my father: to the worm, Thou art my mother, and my sister. And where is now my hope?"

And in a more contemporary vein, the poetry of Gerard Manley Hopkins gives an immediacy and a poignant horror to the anguish of depression:

> "No worst, there is none. Pitched past pitch of grief
> More pangs will, schooled at forepangs, wilder wring."

And he had a warning for us all:

> "Oh the mind, mind has mountains; cliffs of fall,
> Frightful, sheer, no-man-fathomed. Hold them cheap
> May who ne'er hung there."

Not to "hold them cheap" or leave them "no-man-fathomed," but to seek understanding and, through it, relief for depression, is the purpose of the study of the clinical condition.

What does depression look like? How does it feel? What are its effects on people who must live and work with a depressive? The case history that follows describes one of the faces of depression.

She is in her late forties and her dark red hair is lined with a dull grey. All the lines on her face turn downward and her light brown eyes move constantly. She wears a well-cut suit, with a button missing from the cuff, a stain near the shoulder, and creases heavily lined across the skirt against her thighs.

She has been ill before, but for her every time is like the first time.

With her family she is virtually silent, her head is bent down, she recrosses her legs occasionally and smokes incessantly, but otherwise seems still, shrunk into herself. Talk passes over her, but her solid presence demands attention. She will not participate and everyone feels that she must tactfully be encouraged to talk. Everyone tries: a question, a suggestion, a reference to a new book. Then someone mentions the weather. It is a signal: head back, eyes glittering, she creates a silence with a stinging, bitter comment about the weather, a comment designed to convey that there is no one who can understand the effect of cold on her and that implies that the weather is taking a personal stand against her. After the silence, people rush to change the subject, fill in the gap, cover the awkwardness.

Head bent again, her mouth twists constantly, despair and contempt fighting for the upper hand on a once handsome face.

For her, being ill means waking before it is light, a clutching gnawing vague pain inside, the beginnings of a dull headache, and a feeling of terror. Before she is properly awake, she worries that she has overslept, will miss the train, be late for work, has she adequate clothes for the weather, will it snow; then, awake, she feels alone, utterly alone, utterly useless, utterly without value, facing a meaningless day that will be a constant battle with which to cope. The ache seems so bad she thinks she cannot get out of bed; it seems that no one cares whether she lives or dies; she cannot read, she cannot write letters, her bedroom is in a state of shocking disorder but it does not seem worthwhile to tidy it. She stays in bed too long and then, heart pounding, breathing fast, races ineffectually through her morning chores, terrified that she will be late for work, afraid that her son will be late for school, worried that her daughter has not yet picked out a new coat, calculating there is not enough money for it anyway, resentful that the month's support money for the children has not arrived from her ex-husband, hands shaking so that she burns them on the toaster.

By midmorning, the aches have receded. Working, she is distracted, dulled, and able to produce the minimum her job requires although the familiar self-abuse continues.

She made a terrible mistake in moving to this city, she should never have taken the children from their father. If she could work harder she could earn more, they cannot manage on what they have. The climate is unbearable, she could slip and fall on those icy sidewalks at any time, and then what would happen to the children. The children don't love her, they treat her like dirt; other people's children have more time for their parents. Her son might get killed at any minute in an automobile accident and the police would take hours and hours to let her know—they are lazy. She has been a terrible burden to her daughter, a girl ought not to have to cook every night because her mother is too tired.

By the end of the day, she is worn out, she has lived a thousand painful accidents, participated in a thousand deaths, mourned a thousand mistakes. She is exhausted. Back in her house, she stumbles to her bed and collapses. "It's all very well for you," she tells her teenage daughter. "You can stand the weather. Don't cook for me, I'm too ill to eat."

Her behavior takes a heavy toll on everyone around her. Her children have seen it all before, of course, but to them also, every time is like the first time, or worse, because in the back of their minds they remember how she whispered, once, "I can't go on," or raged in a darkened room "you'd be better off without me" and they are nagged by the fear of suicide. They understand that she is ill, but even their understanding and their kindness is drained by the emotional demands that never stop. When she complains for the hundredth time that she has no friends, they remind her of her friends, and she says, "Oh, I suppose so"—and they are irritated and caustic as they try to demonstrate that she is being irrational. They slowly learn that telling her she is irrational is useless, so they take to walking out of the room.

"I don't want you to go out of the house tonight. The temperature is dropping, the roads may freeze, I am afraid of an accident. You can't go out and leave me here terrified about you. It's you I'm thinking of." So they leave the room, furious, self-righteous, helpless, every trivial moment of their lives the focus of a new scene, the occasion for a new set of choices and loyalties.

At work, her competence and her wit at first make her attractive to her colleagues. Then they notice that she is often taking medicine for "the worst headache I've ever had" or for "keeping myself awake after a sleepless night, I really did not sleep one minute"; they see she calls in at the company doctor's office at least once a day; they watch her rage over small slights or sit, crushed, silent, gloomy, for no apparent reason. They hear her on the telephone. "Why are you home so late? I've been calling for 10 minutes to check that you got home alright." They wait for the 20-year-old boy at the other end to speak and then they hear "I didn't say you shouldn't stop for a soda, but you know how I worry until I am sure you are home. You know how I worry." It goes on and on until the women who work with her lose their patience and sympathy, they are tired of it, it drains their emotions and their energy.

On weekends she lies on the bed, staring at the ceiling, tears running down her cheeks, her body heaving intermittently with sobs loud enough to be heard through the large house. Her brother, visiting, tries to divert her. Nothing will. He tries to discuss rationally all the things that are worrying her. As he dismisses each one, as he shows her how each thing is trivial and can be easily handled, she rails at him and in an empty voice says "I suppose so." Then she frightens him more by saying, "I can't cope, I just can't go on."

She is utterly self-absorbed. She cannot discuss anything but her pain and her fears, and when other things are discussed around her, she retreats into the stubborn, accusing silence that embarrasses everyone else. She pours her story out to everyone who will listen, and for a time, most people do, sympathetically and kindly. But her demands are consuming, terribly consuming, not only of time, but of energy and emotion, and people find that they are neglecting things they ought or want to do. Once started, she cannot be stopped: words, problems, judgments, fears, categorical statements, frightened appeals hurtle on.

The most difficult demand for everyone around her is that she simply does not hear what is said to her. She does not want to know what anyone else thinks. It is impossible for her family to have relationships with her. Their posture is that of punching bags. After a few weeks, they are punched limp, drained, exhausted.

She is able to continue working, perhaps because she must; but she is only barely able to hold her job. And at every other level, in all her other roles and relationships, she is utterly incapable of functioning effectively. She cannot make simple choices or trivial decisions; she cannot conduct a conversation or listen to someone else's joys or troubles; she cannot, in fact, cook a meal or change the linen on a bed. She is a physical and emotional drain on everyone around her and the patterns of her thinking and behavior are disrupted and disturbed. She feels desperately unhappy and utterly without hope. She is an acute agitated depressive.

There are many other "faces" of depression; other ways in which it manifests itself clinically—with psychosis, retardation, physical complaints, and poor functioning. These will all be described in more detail later.

‖ *CHAPTER TWO* ‖

CLINICAL FEATURES

The affective disorders take two major forms: depression and mania. This chapter deals with their signs and symptoms.

SYMPTOMS OF DEPRESSION

The central symptoms of depression are sadness, pessimism, and self-dislike, along with a loss of energy, motivation, and concentration. The extent to which these symptoms are present and their combinations are infinitely variable; other symptoms are frequent and sometimes dominate the clinical picture. The signs and symptoms of depression are outlined in Table 1.

Mood

The mood is one of sadness. Patients complain of feeling "blue," miserable, unhappy, "not myself." Depressed patients are unable to respond to the things they usually enjoy. "The pleasure has gone out of life," is at the center of the depressed patient's pervasive feeling of worthlessness, emptiness, and futility.

Many depressed patients cannot account for the fact that they feel sad, although others attribute their condition to specific events. These range from immediate problems in their life situations to fully developed delusionary systems.

TABLE 1: Signs and Symptoms of Depression

Mood
   Sad, unhappy, blue
   Crying

Thought
   Pessimism
   Ideas of guilt
   Self-denigration
   Loss of interest and motivation
   Decrease in efficiency and concentration

Behavior and Appearance
   Neglect of personal appearance
   Psychomotor retardation
   Agitation

Somatic
   Loss of appetite
   Loss of weight
   Constipation
   Poor sleep
   Aches and pains
   Menstrual changes
   Loss of libido

Anxiety Features

Suicidal Behavior
   Thoughts
   Threats
   Attempts

Crying occurs frequently among mildly to moderately depressed people, not only in response to specific experiences, but also because of minor frustrations or when angered, or sometimes even, for no apparent reason. More severely depressed patients may not cry. They say, "If only I could cry," or "I feel as if I want to cry, but I am all dried up inside."

Thought

As depression develops people become increasingly inefficient. Loss of interest, decrease in energy, inability to accomplish tasks, difficulty in concentration, and the erosion of motivation and ambition all combine to impair efficient functioning. For many depressives, the first signs of the illness are in the area of their increasing inability to cope with their work and responsibilities. This may be the only overt manifestation of the illness at first. Consequently, when several months later a patient appears with a full-blown depression and is asked what caused it, he may say that it arose as a result of difficulties experienced at work. A frequent example is a student who blames his depression on having failed recent important examinations, but in fact failed the examinations because of the inefficiency associated with the onset of the depression.

The depressive expresses judgments of himself ranging from inadequacy and inefficiency to extreme guilt. With little or no basis in reality, and showing little or no response to reassurance, argument, or emotional appeal, he denies past achievements and abilities. He regards himself as incompetent at best and disgustingly sinful at worst.

The ideas of incompetence may be limited to one or two aspects of life or may become generalized. Then the depressed patient believes himself to be "no good." A lifetime of efficiency and success become meaningless. He thinks only of failure and worthlessness. If confronted with objective evidence of past achievements, he will reject them as irrelevant or anticipate their immediate disintegration. There is no belief in the reality of past achievements. It is as if he is saying, "How could anyone as useless (or bad) as me have achieved this?"

Ideas of having been wrong and guilt about real or imagined events may increase, together with the belief that justified, inevitable punishment will follow.

A successful dairy farmer worth several hundred thousand dollars stated that the income tax authorities were after him. They would "discover" that he "owed" hundreds of thousands of dollars in back taxes and would, therefore, confiscate all his property. His fears were quite unfounded, but assurances made no difference. He "knew" that he was "no good," and that he had done so much wrong in his life that he was certainly about to lose everything.

He had recently been gored by a bull and believed that this proved that the process of retribution for past sins (all fantasized insofar as we were able to determine) was inevitable.

A few days later he became convinced that the Revenue Department had acted, and that all his property had been confiscated.

Several days later he came to believe that his death was imminent. He was sure that God intended him to die soon. He no longer deserved to live. He saw himself as a burden to his wife and children. No longer was he a man who had provided his family with all possible material comforts.

He was worse than useless to them. He saw himself as a liability. Nothing could persuade him that this was not true.

For others, ideas of guilt may center around real events that become distorted or exaggerated until they are no longer able to distinguish between reality and fantasy. Many women in their 50s and 60s become concerned about masturbation they practiced while they were teenagers, or sexual "indiscretions" of 30 years earlier. They ruminate over these events, exaggerating them in the process. Experiences forgotten for years now become the center of their lives. They believe that they will now be punished for these past "sins" and that there is no salvation. They must "pay the price."

In many cases the severely depressed patient blames himself for events that have nothing at all to do with him. He believes himself responsible for problems other people are having.

Behavior and Appearance

Appearance often signals a depressed person. His sad, unhappy face, dejected attitude, and bowed posture strongly suggest the condition. If it is not immediately apparent, then the typical demeanor of misery appears when the patient begins to talk. While this may be interrupted by an occasional smile, particularly if he thinks that it is expected of him, the smile is usually frozen and superficial and has earned the name "mirthless." Some depressives do hide their despair behind a bland or even a smiling face, although this is unusual.

As the depression deepens there is a progressive loss of concern about personal appearance and grooming. Clothing may be sloppy, creased, and even dirty. Personal hygiene may be neglected. Women normally conscious of their appearance will stop using cosmetics and allow their hair to become tangled and untidy.

Psychomotor retardation is a symptom frequently associated with depression. It involves an apparent inhibition or slowing down of all bodily movements and thinking and a reduction in spontaneous movements and expressive gestures. When the depressed person moves he is frequently slow and deliberate, as if a tremendous effort is involved. Spontaneous speech is reduced; there is little attempt to initiate conversation or engage in discussions. Answers to specific questions are sparse. In very severe cases retardation becomes so marked that the patient becomes mute and almost stuporous and may resemble a catatonic schizophrenic. This is rarely seen today; therapeutic intervention usually aborts the course of the illness before it reaches this stage.

Although psychomotor retardation is widely described both in text-books of psychiatry and in the clinical records of depressed patients, there is some question as to its real extent and significance. Colbert and Harrow (1967) recently studied this phenomenon in a group of hospitalized depressed patients. They defined psychomotor retardation by means of structured clinical interviews and observation and by psychological and performance tests. They suggested that it was neither as severe nor as extensive as the patients and their families reported as characteristic of the patient's prehospital condition. They found that the retardation fluctuated considerably depending on the criteria for measurement and the setting in which it was determined. Furthermore, most of the patients with apparent retardation were capable of mobilizing themselves effectively when they encountered unusual circumstances. To some degree the retardation was related to the age of the patients instead of to their depressed condition.

In contrast, a patient may manifest an *agitated* (rather than retarded) state, and may show extreme restlessness, both physical and psychological. In one such case, for example, a woman patient paces the floor. She sits down, stands up, pulls at her clothes, her hair, wrings her hands, bites her lips, and appears unable to rest for any length of time. Her verbal expressions manifest the same difficulty. She is constantly appealing for help and for reassurance, and like the case described in Chapter One, frantically expresses her anguish and pain. She accosts friends and family, clinging to their arms and asking for help or berating herself and her condition. This type of behavior is frequent among patients who have involutional depression (for a detailed description see page 29).

Somatic Symptoms

There is some evidence that somatic symptoms tend to cluster, a number of them occurring together in the same patient. Among them may be the following.

Loss of Appetite and Weight. Many depressed patients show a marked loss of appetite, particularly as the illness progresses. They do not want to eat, and when they do the food seems tasteless and unpalatable. The loss of appetite (anorexia) may be severe in some depressives. Weight loss is frequent and in some cases may be as much as 30 or 40 pounds in a relatively short period of time. At one time this presented a serious management problem; it was sometimes necessary to tube-feed severely depressed patients to prevent death from the complications of malnutrition. This is rarely necessary today, when it is usually possible to alter the course of the illness by appropriate therapy.

There are some patients for whom the developing depression is accompanied by an increase in appetite. These are usually mildly to moderately depressed.

Constipation. Constipation is frequent in depression. It may become quite severe and the patient may have ten days or more without a bowel movement. The depressive may complain of being "blocked up" or of "rotting inisde."

Sleep Disturbance. Sleep disturbance is a common problem. It is both pervasive and variable. Depressed patients complain of difficulty in falling asleep, frequent restlessness, awaking during the night or in the early hours of the morning, inability to return to sleep, and nightmares. They frequently find that they do not feel rested when they wake up in the morning; they feel that their sleep has been of no benefit to them or that it has been "very light."

There are some people who sleep excessively when depressed. As with depressed patients who eat excessively, the tendency to sleep more usually occurs in milder cases. (The problem of sleep and depression is considered in detail on page 84).

Aches and Pains. Depressed patients complain of physical symptoms affecting every system of the body—including dry mouth, aches and pains, headaches, neuralgia, tight feelings in the chest, and difficulty in swallowing. On occasion one of these complaints may become the dominant symptom (see section on hidden depressions, page 16).

Menstrual Changes. Depressed women frequently report changes in their menstrual cycle. The most frequent problem is a lengthening of the usual cycle, with a much lighter flow. Menstruation may stop completely for several months at a time.

Loss of Libido. Loss of libido is common in depressed patients. This ranges from a decrease in spontaneous interest in sexual activity to a marked aversion for sex.

Anxiety Features

Although sadness is the central mood disturbance, many depressed patients also complain of features of anxiety or other neurotic states. They may complain of tension, uncertainty, vague and nonspecific fears, and a multitude of concerns. They may have the tremor and sweaty palms that are usually associated with an anxiety state.

VARIABILITY OF SYMPTOMS

In some patients symptoms fluctuate considerably over time and according to circumstances. For example, a housewife may be moderately depressed all day but improve considerably in the evening when her husband returns home. Her mood fluctuates in accordance with the amount of support and assistance available. Mood and associated features are intimately related to the environment. Gillespie (1929) termed this *reactivity* or responsivity— the extent of depression is linked directly with the frustrations and rewards of the immediate environment.

The other extreme is *autonomous* depression, where the mood is fixed. No matter where she is, what is happening to her, or whom she is with, the patient's depression remains constant. These patients do not respond to entertainment or diversion and show little change whether they are alone or in company.

Sometimes depressed patients show fluctuations in the form of *diurnal variation*—that is, they feel worst and their symptoms are more pronounced at a constant period in the day, usually the early morning. They may feel very bad on awakening in the morning and not want to get up, finding the idea of the day ahead distressing and impossible. Several hours later there may be some relief in the severity of their symptoms.

The occurrence of diurnal variation suggests that there may be a disturbance in the *circadian rhythm* of depressed patients. The circadian rhythm is the normal 24-hour cycle that marks many bodily functions ranging from the production of some hormones (for example, cortisol) to body temperature. Thus, for instance, we know that the normal body temperature is not 98.4°F throughout the day. It may be as much as one degree higher at 7:00 A.M. than it is at 1:00 or 2:00 A.M. Many basic body functions follow this rhythm, which is fixed and extremely difficult to alter experimentally. Preliminary studies suggest the possibility of an alteration in the normal circadian rhythm of blood level of cortisol in some depressed patients. The normal pattern is altered so that instead of reaching a peak at about 6:00 A. M. these patients show a peak several hours earlier —about 2:00 or 3:00 A. M. Another aspect of the possible disturbance of this basic rhythm might be the tendency for early morning wakening in some depressed patients.

SUICIDAL BEHAVIOR

Incidence

Suicide has become an increasingly important cause of death throughout the world. More than 20,000 people kill themselves each year in the United States, making suicide the eleventh most common cause of death; between the ages of 15 and 44 it is the fourth most common. Furthermore, it is generally accepted that the recorded figures for suicide and suicidal attempts conceal more than they reveal. Although estimates vary, true suicide rates are probably two or three times higher than the reported figures. Furthermore, there are 5 to 10 suicidal attempts for every successful suicide. For a variety of personal, social, and religious reasons, many suicidal attempts are ignored; some are not even recognized. Also, a number of people who die through apparently accidental means, including automobile accidents, may well have killed themselves deliberately.

Relationship with Depression

Although many factors contribute to the development of suicidal thoughts or attempts, it is evident that depression plays a central role in the problem. The ideas of guilt and despair present in the depressive may lead either to the belief that he deserves to die (self-punishment) or that the future is so bleak that he would rather die than live in his present condition (escape).

The exact relationship between depression and suicide is difficult to pinpoint. In a careful study of 134 successful suicides, Robins et al. (1959) found that 94 percent had been psychiatrically ill before committing suicide, and that 45 percent had been depressed. These figures are higher (and probably more accurate) than those reported by other workers because Robins and his associates visited the homes of the suicides soon after the event and did not simply rely on available records. Sainsbury (1968), working in England, suggested that an even higher percentage of successful suicides were suffering from depression.

Furthermore, it is known that alcoholism is the second most frequent condition associated with suicide, and that many alcoholics are also depressed. Thus depression probably plays an important role in this group of suicides as well.

Pokorny (1964) studied the suicide rate over a 15-year period among United States Armed Forces veterans. He found that the suicide rates per 100,000 per year were: for depressed patients, 566; for schizophrenics, 167; for alcoholics, 133; for neurotics, 119; for people with personality disorders, 130; and for people with organic disorders, 78. He compared these findings with the mean-age-adjusted suicide rate among male veterans, which was only 22.7 per 100,000. The suicide rate for depressed patients was 25 times higher than that for the control subjects.

The frequency of suicidal attempts and thoughts among depressed patients is much more difficult to determine than is the actual suicide rate. One survey that we conducted recently suggested that at least 25 percent of hospitalized depressed patients manifest suicidal behavior in the form of thoughts, threats, or attempts.

Robins et al. (1959) have reviewed the literature and suggested that approximately 14 percent of patients with the diagnosis of manic-depressive illness will eventually *commit* suicide. If this is contrasted with the national suicide rate of approximately one in 10,000 (0.01 percent) it is clearly significant.

Depressed patients seldom commit suicide when severely ill. At this stage there may be a profound retardation that inhibits the positive action required for a suicidal attempt. The danger period comes after treatment or partial remission has allowed sufficient lifting of the depression and lightening of the retardation, when the patient has the motivation and energy to make the attempt. It has been observed that suicide rates are particularly high among patients who are allowed out of the hospital on weekend passes or in the first few weeks after discharge. Thus Wheat (1960) found that of a group of psychiatric patients who committed suicide, 30 percent did so while in the hospital and, of those discharged from the hospital, 63 percent did so during the first month.

Although it is difficult to predict suicidal behavior in a particular individual, some general information is available about the characteristics of people who die by suicide.

It is known that women are far more likely to make suicidal attempts than are men. (Likewise, depression is far more common among women than among men.) However, a higher percentage of men than women who make suicidal attempts will die as a result of these attempts. In other words, in general, suicidal threats and attempts are more serious in men than in women.

Suicide is much more common in the elderly than in the middle aged. As the population of elderly people increases, it is likely that the incidence of suicide will also increase. There is evidence that the high incidence of suicide in the elderly is related to the decrease in their meaningful involvement in family and society, and also correlates with a movement away from a familiar environment (Batchelor, 1957). Thus the increasing tendency for people to move away from their lifelong homes for retirement may well lead to an even greater incidence of suicide in this group of people in the future. It has been shown that in communities where the aged maintain an important and revered role in the family and society there is a low incidence of suicide.

This observation of a significant association between aging and social isolation is compatible with theories first presented by Durkheim in 1897. He proposed that there was a positive correlation between the incidence of suicide and the absence of social integration and regulation. Therefore, not only is there an increased incidence of suicide in the isolated elderly, but suicide is also more common in the divorced and separated, the single, and the widowed. Of course, it is quite possible that the association between social isolation and suicide is not a causal one but a reflection of some common underlying condition. However, these factors do serve as additional warnings in individuals who are regarded as suicide risks.

Farberow and Schneidman (1965) have suggested that suicidal behavior constitutes a "cry for help." In other words, the suicidal person is transmitting a desperate message of suffering and anguish to those around him in the hope that they will respond with some relief. It has been shown that the vast majority of people who do kill themselves have given a warning of their intentions. This may take the form of comments to family, friends, a priest, or a physician. Too often this is ignored because of the old maxim that "those who talk do not do"; Of course, not every person who speaks of suicidal intent makes a serious effort. It has been shown that although some people who make suicidal attempts are determined to kill themselves (that is, they may reasonably expect their actions to lead to death), many make a minor and apparently attention-seeking effort. In this latter group the act seems to be directed toward the achievement of some interpersonal effect rather than death. The prototype for this is a hysterical young woman who makes dramatic threats followed by a superficial scratching of her wrist because of a broken love affair. Perhaps she hopes to force her lover to return to her. People who engage in this type of action are not usually seriously depressed.

Contrasted with this is the middle-aged person who is profoundly depressed and believes that he and all associated with him are doomed to suffer a terrible life because of past sins. He proceeds systematically to kill everyone in his family and finally himself. Here there is no equivocation. He kills his wife and children in order to "spare them the terrible suffering" that he believes their future holds.

SEVERITY OF DEPRESSION

The severity of a depression varies widely. Some patients continue to function moderately well, meeting most of their responsibilities with reasonable efficiency. Often their friends, relatives, or colleagues may not be aware that they are experiencing any difficulties, but they have no motivation to do more than is absolutely necessary. Others are totally incapacitated by the depression and may require urgent hospitalization.

The severity of a depression can be defined in several different ways. Consider the following three patients:

1. Mr. A. J., a 42-year-old successful businessman, had no significant psychiatric problem all his life, and suddenly developed a depression. Over a period of several weeks he became progressively more disturbed and immobilized. His illness was marked by severe delusions of guilt, nihilism, and incompetence. He made a serious suicidal attempt by taking a large overdose of drugs and would have died had his family not found him unconscious and transferred him to a hospital. In the hospital he was treated and within a month he was freed of all his symptoms.

2. Mrs. P. H. had been in treatment intermittently for eight years. During this time she had been hospitalized briefly on three occasions. At no time during the eight years had she been completely symptom free. She had a constant feeling of unhappiness and she derived no satisfaction from life. As a consequence, her husband and three children became increasingly estranged from her and her marriage was in jeopardy. She participated in psychotherapy with several therapists as well as having been treated with various antidepressant drugs. None of these had a significant effect.

3. Mr. T. S. was a cyclic depressive. Two or three times a year for about three or four weeks on each occasion he became depressed. Several times he had had to be admitted to hospital for 7 to 10 days. All these episodes have been marked by spontaneous remission.

These three examples illustrate the problem we are considering. Which patient is "more severely ill"? The first, who would have died had there not been rapid intervention, but who is now completely symptom free and whose prognosis is excellent? Mrs. P. H., who has not been free of symptoms for years, the fabric of whose life is disintegrating, and whose prognosis is very poor? Or the third patient, who is able to function reasonably efficiently and enjoy a productive and satisfying life most of the time, but for whom depressive epiodes may be regarded as inevitable, and for whom there is the risk that they will become increasingly frequent or severe and may lead to a suicidal attempt?

Obviously all three of these people are severely ill, but in different ways. There is no practical method (nor need there be) of comparing them with each other.

HIDDEN DEPRESSIONS

A large number of patients for whom the primary problem is depression first complain of symptoms that lead to a diagnosis of physical illness. This problem of hidden depression (*depressive equivalent, masked depression, missed depression,* and *latent depression* are terms sometimes used) is particularly common among patients in their teens and early twenties and in the elderly. Most medical clinics have a group of chronic patients who have been repeatedly investigated for persistent complaints of such problems as headache, abdominal pain or symptoms of gastrointestinal disturbance, lower backache, chronic tiredness, and so forth. Repeated and careful study of these patients reveals no physical basis for their symptoms. A routine interview may not reveal any clear-cut features of depression, or even if a patient does appear unhappy this may be dismissed as an inevitable consequence of the "debilitating illness." Several studies have now shown that for at least some of these patients the primary problem is depression. Meticulous history taking does reveal sufficient evidence to support this diagnosis, and these patients often show a favorable response to specific antidepressant therapy.

The following case histories show two particularly striking examples of this problem.

Mr. A. J. was a 52-year-old man who was referred with a diagnosis of drug addiction. At that time he was taking over 100 analgesic tablets a day because of a severe headache that he had had for about a year. In spite of this extremely large dose of pain-relieving medication, his headache persisted. Originally there had been serious concern about a possible neurological disease such as a brain tumor, and he had been carefully examined for this and other possibilities. All the special investigations that were performed were negative. His physicians then embarked on a series of symptomatic remedies without success. Through this period he began taking increasing amounts of pain-relieving medication and a diagnosis of drug addiction was made. It was suggested that his complaints of headache were spurious attempts to obtain drugs—his real purpose in consulting doctors. When referred for a psychiatric consultation, a careful history revealed a number of symptoms suggestive of an underlying depression, and after talks with both the patient and his family it seemed probable that many of these symptoms had been present at the time of his first complaint of headache and were probably not a consequence of the difficulties that he had had in the past year. On the basis of this investigation, a course of antidepressant therapy was initiated, with no special attention to the headache. There was a complete remission of symptoms after several weeks, and two years later he had not developed any further symptoms.

The second patient, Mr. B. J., was a 50-year-old married man who was admitted to hospital with a diagnosis of cerebral hemorrhage. His symptoms included partial paralysis of both legs and total blindness. It was thought that these symptoms had arisen as a result of a "stroke"—

hemorrhage into areas of the brain responsible for controlling the activities of his legs and his sight. On examination he was a very ill and, significantly, a very withdrawn man. He was mildly depressed, but it was assumed that this was a reasonable consequence of his physical symptoms. However, neurological examination showed that the nature and distribution of the physical symptoms were such that they could not have been caused by a brain hemorrhage. The patient was placed on antidepressant medication and psychotherapy was begun. After several weeks there was some improvement in his physical condition but he had become more depressed. It then emerged that the patient had severe guilt feelings over the death of a friend some 30 years earlier. The boy had died in a traffic accident and the patient had been blamed for it; many of the details of the experience as well as his own emotional reactions to it had been repressed. However, on four occasions since then he had developed fairly clear-cut depressions. Each successive episode had been a little more bizarre and had featured an increasing number of physical symptoms. Exploration of this problem with the patient, together with the antidepressant medication, brought about a rapid relief of symptoms—both emotional and physical—and within two months he was discharged from the hospital symptom free. It would seem reasonable to assume that the gross physical symptoms with which he had been admitted were, in fact, part of a depression.

It must be emphasized that not all patients with physical complaints for which no organic cause can immediately be demonstrated are suffering from a depression. From time to time there is a sober reminder of this when a patient diagnosed as depressed and given electroconvulsive therapy dies as a result of hemorrhage into and around a brain tumor. The tumor, clinically unrecognized, had manifested the symptoms of depression.

The frequency of hidden depression is difficult to determine. It is possible that many tens of thousands of people with minor somatic complaints may in fact be mildly depressed. Several studies (Dowling & Knox, 1964; Lesse, 1968) of patients in general medical wards suggest that about 20 percent of them are depressed; however, this figure does not distinguish between those for whom the depression is primary and perhaps underlying the physical symptoms that led to hospitalization, and those who are depressed as a result of the physical illness and hospitalization.

One way in which depression is frequently masked is by the excessive use of alcohol or drugs. Although not all alcoholics and drug addicts have developed these conditions as a result of depression, a considerable number, especially in the middle years of life, have turned to alcohol or drugs in an attempt to escape the pervasive misery of depression. A vicious cycle is established early in the development of the illness. The patient, feeling somewhat low and miserable, finds that a few drinks tend to improve his mood. With time and the development of his depression, he needs more and more alcohol to relieve his painful, sad feelings. After a while the underlying mood may be forgotten or disguised. When the patient eventually seeks help he may be regarded simply as an alcoholic instead of as a person whose primary problem of depression has been complicated by the excessive use of alcohol. This distinction is of crucial importance because the treatment will be quite different depending on the diagnosis. The case history of Mr. A. J. on page 17 serves as an example.

SYMPTOMS OF MANIA

Mood

A change of mood in the direction of elation is the central feature of mania. This elation is out of proportion to reality; at times it may be completely inappropriate. Hypomania is a mild form of mania. An example of mania is a patient who has recently lost his job and depleted his financial resources as a result of a manic episode, but continues to be totally unconcerned, happy-go-lucky, and carefree. He has no doubt about his ability to handle successfully all problems confronting him. He has ideas of omnipotence, of being attractive, desirable, and efficient. Elation and overconfidence are dominant, but fluctuate. If he feels himself pressed or opposed too vigorously, the manic patient will become very angry, aggressive, and irritable. If he does not feel that he is being interfered with or opposed, his joy often transmits itself to those around him. Even clinicians, aware of the patient's condition, are caught up in his infectious good humor. It is commonplace to see smiling faces among the staff after brief interviews with manic patients; however, lengthier interviews often lead to friction and irritation.

In a mild form this elation may serve the patient well. Thus, for example, a mildly hypomanic salesman may be very successful as a result of his ability to convey his enthusiasm to clients. In social situations the hypomanic is often extremely warmly regarded and may find himself very popular, again as a result of his infectious good spirits. It is possible that many successful people are chronically mildly hypomanic; their ability to achieve a great deal in a relatively short space of time, to appear indefatigable, and to be able to ignore adversity may often be the result of mild hypomania.

Thought

Changes in a patient's thinking become more central as the manic process develops. His thoughts flit from one subject to another. Inconsequential stimuli are elaborated into irrelevant new themes and there is often difficulty in maintaining a flow of thought along defined lines. Usually there is an apparent, although not necessarily substantial, logical link between the rapid sequence of thoughts and ideas expressed by manic patients. In contrast, the disordered thoughts of a schizophrenic patient do not usually have this quality, although disjointed ideas will seem logical to him.

The flight of ideas of mania manifests itself not only in rapid changes in thought content but also in rapid speech. In the midst of the logorrhea (rapid outpouring of words) there are frequent attempts at jokes, puns, and clang associations. Lorenz (1953) has studied the speech patterns of manic patients and reported on several significant departures from the average: increased use of pronouns and verbs; decreased use of adjectives; and a high verb-adjective quotient.

The manic may have ideas of grandiosity; potency, wealth, power, perception are all claimed. He perceives his everyday achievements as remarkable and speaks eloquently about them. He goes to considerable lengths to prove his claims if he is challenged, but becomes angry if he suspects that serious doubts are being cast on them.

Motor Activity

There is usually a marked increase in motor activity. The manic is restless when confined. He seeks exaggerated and unnecessary forms of motor activity—he speaks loudly, finds excuses to break into song, and works energetically, though generally ineffectively. In more severe cases there may be states of manic excitement in which there are bursts of apparently purposeless activity. The manic patient may scream, curse, and become violent under these conditions. He is seemingly tireless and will engage in hours of activity that would usually exhaust him in a short time. He sleeps and eats much less than usual.

Clayton, et al. (1965) analyzed the frequency of occurrence of these symptoms in a group of 31 manic patients. They found that hyperactivity, flight of ideas, and pressure of speech were present in 100 percent of the patients; euphoria and distractability in 97 percent; circumstantiality (talking around the point) in 96 percent; decreased sleep in 94 percent; grandiosity and/or religiosity in 79 percent; ideas of reference (interpreting neutral events as having relevance to himself) in 77 percent; increased sexuality in 74 percent; and delusions in 73 percent.

CHAPTER THREE

CLASSIFICATION OF DEPRESSION: MAJOR SYNDROMES

MANIC-DEPRESSIVE ILLNESS

In 1851 the French psychiatrist Jules Falret first described *la folie circulaire,* and in 1863 a German psychiatrist, Karl Kahlbaum, coined the term *cyclothymia*. Kraepelin expanded the concept in 1896 and proposed the term manic-depressive psychosis, which included all the "periodic and circular insanities, mania, melancholia, and some cases of amentia." He later expanded this concept to incorporate all cases of "affective excess." Kraepelin justified this amalgamation on the grounds that they all involve a mood disturbance, are difficult to distinguish from each other, seem to occur in the same patient at different times, and have a uniformly good prognosis.

For a long time in the United States the term manic-depressive *psychosis* was replaced by the term manic-depressive *reaction*. This was because of the influence of the doyen of American psychiatry, Adolf Meyer, who proposed that psychiatric disorders constitute a reaction to experiences and events instead of a precise, encapsulated disease process.

Until recently manic-depressive illness was classified as "functional" by the American Psychological Association. This meant that "no matter what the complex causality of the disorder may be, it is the particular form of functioning (or of operating) with its content that constitutes the predominant and primary (although not exclusive) essence of the disorder and leads to secondary sequelae, both organic and functional" (Arieti, 1959).

In 1969 the term manic-depressive *illness* was adopted by psychological and psychiatric associations in order to bring the American classification into line with that of the World Health Organization. This change reflected the increasing realization that organic factors may play an important (but not necessarily exclusive) part in the etiology of manic-depressive illness.

Today the term manic-depression should be used to refer to a person who has had one or more episodes of depression or mania without apparent cause. The terms *endogenous depression* and *cyclic depression* are sometimes used synonymously with manic-depression.

Course of Manic-Depressive Illness

The form of the illness ranges from a single nonrecurring episode of either depression or mania, through recurrent depressive episodes, to a cyclic illness in which there are successive periods of depression and mania following each other immediately. The length of any episode may range from hours to weeks, months, or even years.

The first clear-cut episodes usually occur in the patients' early thirties. Careful observation may reveal that there were significant fluctuations in mood at an earlier age than this, but it is unusual for a clear-cut episode of manic-depressive illness to occur in the teens or early twenties.

On the basis of one or two episodes it is not possible to predict the future pattern of the illness because it is very idiosyncratic; in some people it will follow a random course and in others it may develop with cyclic regularity. Cases have been reported of patients with manic-depressive illness who alternate between manic and depressive episodes every 24 hours for months on end. In some the alteration between the two mood phases is so precise that it occurs at a regular time of day—particularly in the early morning. In other patients there may be a seasonal pattern to the mood swings, and in still others an annual pattern. Many patients will have stable periods between the recurrent depressive or depressive and manic periods.

Usually the onset of a new episode is not related to any specific environmental stress, although the patient may report such an association. With this condition it is usually apparent that similar stresses have occurred at other times in the patient's life and have not precipitated a pathological mood state.

Individual episodes of depression (or mania) may develop very insidiously. During the first few weeks there is often considerable fluctuation before the course of the illness becomes established and the patient follows a steady downhill course. The degree of disturbance will vary considerably from patient to patient, and indeed for the same patient from time to time. For some the mood disturbance, although clear-cut, is relatively mild and, aside from the subjective disability and discomfort, does not lead to major incapacitation. For others there will be a total disability.

A natural resolution of an episode (rarely seen today because of the widespread use of physical therapies for this condition) will follow a similar course to the onset. The recovery process fluctuates considerably at first, from day to day and even on the same day. In general, the prognosis for an individual episode is good, even without treatment, provided that the patient does not commit suicide. Although Kraepelin regarded manic-depressive illness as a self-limiting condition, as opposed to the chronic deteriorating process of schizophrenia, it has been observed that a small number of patients with manic-depressive illness develop a chronic condition in later life. It is of course possible that the patients who become chronically ill were incorrectly diagnosed in the first place; they may have been suffering from schizophrenia all along.

Relationship Between Mania and Depression

The majority of manics have a history of previous episodes of depression. For example, Clayton et al. (1965) found that 22 of 31 patients studied had a previous history of depression. It is reasonable to assume that some of the other nine manic patients would develop depressive episodes sometime in the future.

Mania is frequently regarded as the mirror image or polar opposite of depression. Certainly from the behavioral point of view this is a reasonable conclusion. Both the mood and behavior of manics are apparently opposite of that seen in depression; sadness gives way to apparent joy and apathy to excitement and drive. It has been widely suggested that mania represents a defense against a developing or underlying depression. According to this theory the depression is so painful that the individual unconsciously denies these feelings and instead develops the mania. Further, some patients have clinical features of both mania and depression at the same time. For example, an obviously manic person may break into tears while discussing his problems. It is as if the tears are just below the surface of his excited "high" state and the change occurs in seconds. This implies that the conceptualization of mania and depression as polar opposites is an oversimplification.

An increasing amount of evidence (much of it preliminary) suggests that changes in physiological functioning in manics and depressives may be very similar. This includes changes in sleep patterns, in the distribution of sodium in the body, and possibly in the response to some drugs (see Chap-

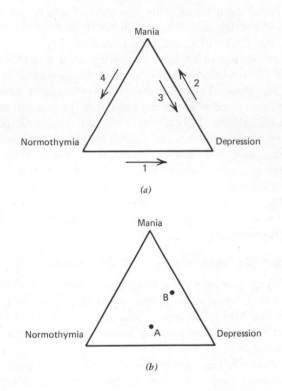

FIGURE 1.   Relationship between mania and depression.

ters 7 and 8 for more details of these changes).

The frequent admixture of symptoms (especially the presence of depressive symptoms in manic patients) and physiological changes suggest that conceptualizing mania and depression as polar opposites may not be correct. An alternative method of understanding their relationship is suggested in Figure 1, where "normal" mood (*normothymia*), depression, and mania are represented as the three corners of a triangle—presenting a variety of options for the development of an affective disorder. For example, in Figure 1a, an individual initially at the "normal" point of the triangle might move directly along the side of the triangle (arrow 1) as he becomes depressed. Such a patient would manifest a definite depression. He might then move in the direction of arrow 2, from a depressed to a manic state. In a cyclic manic-depressive this could follow immediately. The patient's condition would vary depending on where he was "located"; shortly after leaving depression (following arrow 2) he would be predominantly depressed, although there would be some signs of change. Later there would be an admixture of the symptoms of depression and mania, and still later there would be a clear-cut manic episode. This same patient might then follow arrow 3 and re-enter a depressive episode or follow arrow 4 and return to normothymia.

Other patients might move from normothymia to various points within the triangle. Depending on the point at which they settled at the height of their illness they would be predominantly depressed, predominantly manic, or show a mixture of the symptoms of the two states. Thus, for example, patient A in Figure 1b would probably be moderately depressed and not show any significant features of mania. However, patient B might be severely ill, with a mixed syndrome with features of both states. From this model it is obvious that the signs and symptoms usually associated with either depression or with mania may occur together in a wide range of combinations.

Cyclothymic Personality (Affective Personality)

This behavior pattern is manifested by recurring and alternating periods of depression and elation. Periods of elation may be marked by ambition, warmth, enthusiasm, optimism, and high energy. Periods of depression may be marked by worry, pessimism, low energy and a sense of futility. These mood variations are not readily attributable to external circumstances.

(American Psychiatric Association, 1968)

Cyclothymia is essentially a mild version of manic-depressive illness; the clinical features associated with either mania or depression are present in a reduced form. Fluctuations of mood from mild hypomania to mild depression may occur daily, weekly, monthly, or at longer intervals. These intervals are often fairly consistent for any one individual, although variations do occur. There may be intervals of normal mood between the mood swings, or they may go directly from one to the other. Often these changes are relatively slight and although the individual concerned is aware of them he does not regard them as constituting an abnormality. For some cyclothymic personalities these relatively minor mood swings gradually merge into a more severe form and assume the proportions of manic-depressive illness. Others never develop the full-blown condition. It is obviously impossible to draw a strict dividing line between manic-depressive illness and cyclothymia.

REACTIVE DEPRESSION

Reactive depression is a term widely used to describe a depressive condition that arises in association with stressful experiences in a predisposed individual. The nature of the predisposing factor may be either constitutional or psychodynamic. These will be discussed later (page 28).

Gutheil (1959) defines reactive depression as "an acute feeling of despondency and dysphoria of varying intensity and duration. As the name indicates it is not an illness but a reaction, a response to conditions of loss and disappointment. This response is highly subjective; what depresses one individual may leave another unaffected."

The problem of reactive depression is in some ways closely related to everyday grief, mourning, and sadness. These experiences are almost universal; for example, in most societies it is regarded as appropriate to be sad and to mourn the death of a close family member. This is a normal reaction. However, if this mourning should become exaggerated—either in intensity or duration—it is then inappropriate and pathological. Obviously, these normal and pathological mourning responses merge into each other. The decision as to what is an exaggeration of the depression following the loss of a loved one is subjective. Freud in his monograph "Mourning and Melancholia" (1917) suggested that an important distinction between normal grief and depression is the "fall in self-esteem" that occurs in the latter condition.

Reactive depression involves an experience in which a predisposed individual suffers a loss (either real or symbolic) of a loved object. We therefore need to consider both the conditions that might predispose an individual to respond in this way and the nature of the precipitating factors.

Predisposing Factors

There are several ways in which an individual might develop a predisposition to reactive depression. These suggestions are of course not mutually exclusive, and it is probable that several of them are present in any individual. They include the following.

1. Genetic factors (discussed in Chapter 9).

2. Presence of a "depressed personality." Laughlin (1956) described the characteristics of the individual whom he believes is likely to develop a reactive depression. These characteristics include several groups of traits: (a) Depressive, overserious, dependable, studious, conscientious, restricted sense of humor, gloomy, and subdued; (b) increased vulnerability to rejection, disappointment, being let down and frustrated (Laughlin suggested that this relates to an overwhelming unconscious need for love and an intense desire to be dependent); (c) traits suggesting that the person denies and hides from himself all feelings of anger and hostility. These include compliance, conciliation, overpoliteness, subservience, and obsequiousness; (d) features of the obsessive-compulsive personality, including meticulousness, rigidity, perfectionism, and concern with detail.

3. Special childhood losses or stresses occurring at crucial periods of development, which sensitize the individual to depression in later life. The occurrence in adult life of similar losses or stresses (real or symbolic) will reactivate the feelings that prevailed at the time of the original stress, with the consequent development of a reactive depression. For example, the loss of a mother at the age of one or two years will produce feelings of anger and despair at that time in a child. The premature loss of a spouse at a later time will cause not only the inevitable mourning associated with that event, but also a reactivation of the childhood loss and more powerful feelings of anger and despair.

4. The development of a condition in which a response (often inappropriate) "I am no good" occurs after a variety of stimuli. For example, parents might frequently have berated a child for being "stupid" and "clumsy." The child would have learned rapidly that this reflected a poor judgment of himself and would have come to regard himself as "bad." This "bad" self-concept and self-blame might then have become incorporated into his personality. Later in life he would interpret a wide variety of stimuli as rejecting, insulting, or critical, and would activate the original childhood feeling "I am bad," with the consequent development of a depression. Faced with relatively minor frustrations or failures, which most people can easily dismiss, this person would regard them far more seriously and develop an exaggerated reaction.

This condition may be described as a relative deficiency in ego strength with an undue and exaggerated dependence on emotional support from people, work situations, and other sources. There are limited personality resources, and it seems that these people only function well if there is a constant input of love, support, and assurance. Consequently, their relationships are extremely limited both in number and depth. They are sometimes described as "inadequate personalities," and are generally immature and go through life requiring unusually intense dependency relationships. A withdrawal of their sources of support (real or symbolic) may give rise to a depression. This is thought to be based on the intense anxiety that arises as a result of the loss of what Freud termed "narcissistic supplies"—emotional support and reassurance. Such people will show a rapid response with resolution of the depressed mood as soon as they can reconstitute previously disrupted dependency relationships or form new ones.

Precipitating Factors

The other half of the equation concerning the onset of a reactive depression is the presence of a precipitating factor. The precipitating factor most frequently invoked is the loss of an important love object. This loss may be real (death of a spouse) or symbolic (loss of an apparently innocuous object that the patient associates with an important person in his life, about whom he feels ambivalence and guilt).

Many people with an apparently reactive depression have reported that the onset of the depression was associated with certain specific environmental events. However, the fact that a patient reports an association between a stressful life experience and the onset of an illness, and that he believes the two to be associated, does not in itself constitute proof that the reported stress caused the illness. Several explanations must be considered:

1. The stress is a temporal coincidence. We all experience difficulties and strains in the course of everyday living, and only a minority of us develop symptoms sufficiently severe after such experiences to bring them to a psychologist or a psychiatrist. It is therefore possible that the stress events that the patient associates with the onset of his illness are unrelated to the illness.

2. The so-called stress event may arise as a consequence of the illness. This is exemplified in a man who explains his depression as a result of having recently lost an important position. Careful notice might reveal that he had lost his position because of increasing inefficiency associated with the earlier onset of the depression.

3. The stress experience may interact with an underlying predisposing factor or in some way activate a latent problem in a vulnerable personality.

4. The stress event may, in fact, have been the major cause of the depression, either because of the nature or the intensity of the stress. An example would be a woman who is depressed because her husband and children were all killed in a motor accident.

Thus, while there is often no definite causal relationship between adverse environmental events and the onset of a reactive depression, there is no doubt that for many individuals the onset is related in some way to adverse circumstances. We are far from understanding the exact nature of this relationship. Often an individual has had similar experiences at other times in his life without becoming depressed, and there are many people with apparently similar personalities who do not become depressed on exposure to such events. Further study is required for clarification of these complex relationships.

SUCCESS DEPRESSION

Also described as a reactive depression is the apparent paradox of the "depression of success," in which a person who has devoted a great deal of time and effort toward achieving a particular goal becomes depressed after that goal is achieved. At times the depression may be very severe. There are several ways in which this paradoxical situation might arise; among the alternatives are the following.

1. A person may be intimidated by the responsibilities of this newly achieved position; he may be afraid to assume them and as a consequence become depressed.

2. People who are prone to depressive reactions are often extremely dependent individuals. Having achieved success and authority, it is no longer possible to hope for a dependency position and they therefore become depressed.

3. The success may be accompanied by a feeling of "I do not deserve this, I am not good enough." As noted earlier in this chapter, people who become depressed often have poor self-esteem and may not believe that the achievement is in proportion to their abilities.

4. This type of depression may arise because an individual has unconsciously "destroyed" a competitive love object—a parent or sibling. The achievement of success is unconsciously interpreted as victory over the early rival. This victory is unacceptable at a conscious level because it engenders severe guilt feelings, and a depression develops.

5. It is also frequently observed that people become depressed after achieving long-sought-after goals; this arises from an emotional and physical let down, which Nietzsche described as "the melancholia of everything completed."

INVOLUTIONAL MELANCHOLIA

Involutional melacholia, also called *involutional psychotic reaction, involutional behavior disorder,* and *middle-age depression,* occurs during the involutium. This is the period of life between the ages of 40 and 55, which, in women, is associated with certain specific endocrine [1] changes resulting in the menopause. The nature of the endocrine changes occurring in men at this time has not been as clearly defined.

It is also a time of life frequently associated with characteristic changes in family status and in sociocultural relationships. For a woman, it usually marks the stage of life when her children, to whom she may have devoted a major portion of her time, become independent and prepare to leave the home; at the same time, childbearing is no longer possible for her. She must find a new role. Simultaneously, changes in endocrine physiology lead to a cessation of ovulation and menstruation and other bodily changes. For many women this represents a period of crisis and a landmark in the process of aging. They develop doubts about their sexual attractiveness and realize that they have lost their youth. (Paradoxically, for some women sexual satisfaction is increased at this time because of the removal of the fear of pregnancy.)

This is also a stage in which many people find themselves taking stock. After 20 years or more of adult life, there is frequently a questioning of role and purpose, and the realization that many ambitions have not been fulfilled and are unlikely to be. Most people have by this time reached their maximum growth potential. Although for many this is satisfying, and the prospect of continuing along similar lines remains attractive, there are some to whom it is an extremely frustrating experience. They are unwilling and unable to accept that their lifelong ambitions (often unrealistic) will not be achieved. They find themselves angry at their present life situation, and they blame themselves or others for what they perceive as life's limitations and disappointments. This applies especially to the unmarried and childless. All this may be experienced as a loss.

Although many patients who appear for treatment at this time of life do have this background, and attribute their problems to it, it is necessary to be cautious about attributing specific causal significance to either the endocrine changes or to the emotional responses to the changing situation. There are many more people undergoing the same changes who do not develop a psychiatric illness than there are those who do. One way of understanding this is to consider the possibility that these middle-life experiences provide a trigger for an underlying predisposition that now manifests itself. Previously sustained by ambition, optimism, the emotional satisfactions and demands from children, and good health, the susceptible individual, now threatened with isolation and purposelessness and un-

---

[1] The endocrine glands such as the adrenal cortex, thyroid, ovaries, and testes release the hormones they have manufactured directly into the blood stream, allowing a rapid distribution of the hormones throughout the body. They thus affect many different tissues and organs.

dergoing physical changes, develops a psychiatric illness.

Descriptions of this condition usually emphasize women. In part this stems from the commonly held belief (probably untrue) that there is no menopause, no specific physical change to mark this stage of life in men. However, there is probably a male climacteric syndrome that parallels the female menopause. It is apparent, though, that the impact of sociocultural and personal events at this time of life is different for men than for women. A woman's role changes as her children mature and leave home, whereas a man, although affected by this, will continue with his primary task—his work—for many years. Obviously other issues are involved as well. For example, the nature of the hormonal changes that take place in men at this time of life have not been studied in as much detail as they have been in women.

It is possible that a susceptibility to the development of involutional melancholia may result either from a genetic predisposition or from the presence of a particular personality type.

Genetic Predisposition. There is some evidence that genetic (hereditary) factors predispose people to the development of involutional melancholia. For example, it has been shown that if one of a set of identical twins has an involutional psychiatric illness, there is a 60 percent chance that the second one will also develop such an illness (Stenstedt, 1959). The percentage is much lower in nonidentical twins. As identical twins have the same genetic makeup and nonidentical twins do not, this finding strongly suggests a hereditary factor in the development of involutional melancholia.

Premorbid Personality. It is a frequent clinical observation that people who develop involutional psychiatric disorders are obsessional, rigid, and highly moralistic. They are perfectionists who lead narrow lives filled with an exaggerated concern for being on time, doing the "right thing," and always "meeting their responsibilities." They have a limited capacity for relaxation and emotional expression, and function as if their emotions are under a constant restraint. They are often highly regarded because they can always be relied on. They have been described as anal-erotic personalities by some writers. It has been suggested that the development of an involutional illness in these people is partly because of a failure of their defense mechanisms at this time of life, when the specific strains (external and internal) cause a breakdown in their usual methods of adjustment, with a consequent emergence of symptoms. Conclusive evidence of a significant association between involutional melancholia and this personality type is lacking. It is possible that the accounts given by these patients of their previous personalities are highly colored by the illness itself and are therefore distorted to some degree.

Clinical Features

Patients with an involutional psychiatric illness are usually in an agitated depressive state with a considerable amount of hypochondriacal concern and paranoid delusions.

The patient, usually a middle-aged woman, may be somewhat overweight and dowdy in appearance. Typically her hair is unkempt, she does not use cosmetics, and she looks drawn and haggard. She is restless and may pace back and forth. She complains to all who will listen and often to those who would rather not. The complaints often become threats, either toward herself or to others. She demands endless attention, and if she does not receive it from one person, she goes to another. Initially, she may complain that she is not understood, appreciated, or wanted. This may develop into extensive statements about her personal unattractiveness. She portrays herself as justifiably unwanted because of real or imagined wrongdoings and deficiencies in character or body. Hypochondriacal complaints and somatic delusions frequently develop. She may complain of a multitude of aches and pains of a nonspecific nature, of exhaustion, or inability to get out of bed and do anything—even while she is restlessly pacing back and forth. She may become convinced that she is suffering from some dreadful disease, often associated with bowel or reproductive organs. Physical examinations and special investigations, although negative, do not reassure her. In some patients paranoid features dominate.

These patients also show many of the signs and symptoms, described earlier, associated with depression: sleep disturbance, loss of appetite, loss of weight, constipation, suicidal preoccupation, and so on.

Without specific treatment, as was often necessarily the case before the development of physical therapies, this condition was often protracted, and many patients committed suicide or recovered slowly after several years.

It was probably patients of this type, coming to mental hospitals and clinics at the turn of the century, who led diagnosticians to label the condition "involutional psychotic reaction." However, during the involutium many people develop less severe psychiatric symptoms that do not warrant the designation psychotic. They frequently complain of tiredness, minor sleep difficulties, loss of interest, severe boredom, and dissatisfaction with many aspects of their lives. They may be restless and hypochondriacal. Many do not seek help or they may consult a general practitioner whose treatment may be symptomatic. Although there is no formal diagnostic category in which to place these people, it does seem reasonable to regard them as suffering from a mild form of involutional melancholia.

The official classification of psychiatric disorders (APA, 1968) separates involutional melancholia from other forms of depression, with the specific stricture that this term be used only after "all other affective disorders have been ruled out." That is, diagnoses such as manic-depressive illness and reactive depression should be considered and specifically excluded before involutional melancholia is diagnosed. Criteria commonly used to distinguish involutional melancholia from the other affective disorders include the absence of a previous depressive episode, agitation instead of retardation, an insidious onset, and an obsessive-compulsive premorbid personality. However, it is obvious that these features are not unique to this condition.

In the author's opinion there is little rational basis for using a separate diagnostic category simply on the basis of the age of onset of the illness. Either the patients who become psychiatrically ill at this time of life have a distinct illness that is determined by specific sociocultural, hormonal, and/or genetic factors, or their problems are minor variants of the broader categories of depression or schizophrenia. Preliminary studies have suggested that patients with an initial diagnosis of involutional melancholia or involutional psychotic reaction *do* develop psychiatric illnesses, often depressive in type, later in life. Could they then be said to have suffered two episodes of involutional psychotic reaction? Or is the second illness different from the first? Or are both illnesses just episodes in a disorder that is not specifically related to the involutium? It seems likely that we are simply dealing with a variety of depression, the presentation of which is affected by the patient's age and situation in life.

CHAPTER FOUR

CLASSIFICATION OF DEPRESSION: DEVELOPMENT AND APPLICATION

The application of the standard classification of depression outlined in the Appendix and described in Chapter 3 on manic-depressive illness, involutional melancholia, and reactive depression is often unsatisfactory. Each psychologist and psychiatrist has his individual understanding of these terms and uses his own definitions (often poorly articulated). As a result, the rate of agreement between clinicians on the diagnosis of any individual patient is poor: just over 50 percent in several controlled studies.

Some workers hold the view that the classification of psychiatric illness serves no purpose. For example, Karl Menninger (1963) has argued that classifying psychiatric patients is both unscientific and unnecessary. He suggests that all mental illnesses are essentially the same and differ only in degree and form.

Certainly numerous patients have a symptomatology that is either so poorly defined or so complex that the selection of an accurate diagnosis is extremely difficult and depends on the fluctuations at a particular moment. However, difficulties in themselves are not sufficient reason to discard classification.

Classification is an essential step in the development of new concepts of psychological disorders. It is an important method of identifying those features that certain patients have in common, as well as those that distinguish them from each other. Failure to recognize factors that bind patients together in a single class may lead to fruitless efforts and substantial errors. For example, had we simply taken 100, or even 1000, people with mental deficiency and placed them all on a phenylalanine-free diet, the response would have been insignificant and the diet would have been discarded as a treatment. It was first necessary to recognize a subtype of mental deficiency, *phenylketonuria,* and then subject the value of a phenylalanine-free diet to investigation in this specific population, for whom it has been shown to have value in preventing the development of mental deficiency.

Similarly, if the response of an unselected group of 100 depressed patients to a new treatment is studied, and if only 20 of these patients respond favorably, the response may be regarded as therapeutically insignificant; the improvement may be labeled a natural remission or a placebo response and the treatment discarded. However, if we assume that depression is a heterogeneous group of conditions, it is possible that the favorable response of some or all of the 20 patients may have been a specific effect on a condition shared only by those 20 patients and not by the other 80 in the group—although all 100 were depressed. Although it would be necessary to demonstrate this in appropriately controlled trials, the question could not even arise without acceptance and use of methods of classification.

Such an approach does not preclude the desirability of studying depression along other dimensions: as a manifestation of a disturbance in interpersonal relationships, as an abnormal learning pattern, as a distortion of perception, and so on. Only by integrating the information obtained by these various approaches can we hope to extend our understanding of the affective disorders.

HISTORICAL DEVELOPMENT

The historical development of the classification of depression and current attempts to reclassify it illustrate the origin of some of the contemporary difficulties and also suggest lines of further investigation.

When Kraepelin coined the term *manic-depressive psychosis* in 1896, he included "the whole domain of the so-called periodic and circular insanities, mania, a greater part of the morbid states termed melancholia, and also, not an inconsiderable number of cases of amentia." He later expanded the concept to include all cases of "affective excess." Kraepelin in part based his approach to this problem on his etiological classification of exogenous illness, those that were caused by bacterial, chemical, or other toxins, and endogenous illnesses, which he assumed to be caused by degenerative or hereditary disorders. Thus, he wrote, "the principal demarcation in etiology is, above all, between internal and external causes. The two major groups of diseases, exogenous and endogenous, are thus naturally divided" (Kraepelin, 1913).

This perpetuated a nature-nurture division in the understanding of depression. In Kraepelin's view, it was very much an either/or concept. He proposed that manic-depressive psychosis was an endogenous illness and that it was "to an astonishing degree independent of external influences." This led to a confusion of Kraepelin's descriptive observations with a concept of etiology (causation). The extrapolation of observable behavior and subjective reports of mood state and cognition to etiology is unrealistic, and constitutes one source of our current difficulties both in arriving at an acceptable classification for the affective disorders and in developing research into etiology.

Lange (1928) elaborated on Kraepelin's dichotomy. He proposed that, in addition to the endogenous or manic-depressive illness and exogenous depressions, mixed forms could occur, with either the endogenous or exogenous component dominating. He termed the group of endogenous depressions that followed some environmental stress *reactive*.

Several years later Gillespie (1929), a leading British psychiatrist, studied a group of depressed patients and proposed that there were three types of depression: *reactive; autonomous* (independent of environmental stimuli); and *involutional*. There was no difference in the frequency of precipitating factors between the reactive and autonomous groups. The main differentiating factor was *reactivity:* reactive patients showed emotional response to environmental changes, contrasted with the lack of responsiveness shown by autonomous patients.

Gillespie did not attribute any etiological significance to the term reactive. However, when his proposals became integrated with those of Kraepelin, the autonomous group was equated with the endogenous or manic-depressive psychosis, and the reactive group with the exogenous. Here again etiological and descriptive concepts were confused, and were used interchangeably, with the result that diagnoses based on observable behavior or subjective reports of how depressives feel came to include unsubstantiated implications as to its cause.

This confusion was compounded in the 1940s when the increasing use of electroconvulsive therapy (ECT) for depression led to the practice of classifying depressed patients according to whether they responded to this kind of treatment, and with it a changing concept of endogenous depression. It was argued that patients with endogenous depression responded much more favorably to ECT than did patients with reactive depression. However, the patients who responded well to ECT did not always fit

Kraepelin's criteria for endogenous depression or manic-depressive psychosis.

Then it was suggested that if endogenous depression responded best to physical treatment (ECT), and exogenous (or reactive) depression responded best to psychotherapy, then, *ipso facto,* endogenous depression was an organic disorder and reactive depression a psychological disorder. Thus the therapeutic and phenomenological classifications assumed major etiological implications, adding considerably to the confusion.

CONTEMPORARY PROPOSALS

The difficulties of classification have led some workers to propose alternative methods of describing depressed patients.

Symptomatic Approach

As part of the attempt to improve systems of classifying depressed patients there is an increasing tendency to adopt a symptomatic approach. This approach has developed partly because many treatments currently employed seem directed against symptoms irrespective of their origin, instead of against disease entities. Terms such as *target symptoms* and *key symptoms* have come into use. Sainz and Bigelow (1961) studied the response of a group of depressed patients to several different therapies: psychotherapy, electroconvulsive therapy, and an antidepressant drug. Sainz and Bigelow pointed out that "regardless of the apparent homogeneity of the sample, therapeutic results continue to be non-uniform . . . As a natural corollary it seems impossible to escape the further conclusion that equal symptomatology can be—and is—produced by different causes."

Depressive Functional Shift

Depressive functional shift is a term that Pollitt (1965) has used to describe the following group of clinical features: early morning wakening; symptoms worse in the early morning; loss of appetite and loss of weight; loss of sexual desire; constipation; limited emotional facial expression; inability to cry; dry mouth; coldness of the extremities; dryness of the skin. This list of symptoms overlaps considerably with that used to describe endogenous depression.

Pollitt proposed that depressed patients be classified according to the presence (*somatic* or *S* type) or absence (*justified* or *J* type) of the depressive functional shift. The *J* type of depression, he feels, is essentially a "psychological stress, and understandable in terms of the patient's predicament." This diagnosis is only reached if all features of the functional shift are excluded. The *S* type is a "physiological depression," characterized by the presence of the above-listed physical symptoms, which he suggests are not seen collectively in any other illness.

The value of Pollitt's proposals has still to be determined. The suggestion that the presence or absence of "somatic" features can be used as an absolute criterion for diagnosis seems unrealistic. No allowance is made for the possibility that the *S* type might simply be a severe version of the *J* type or that the difference is primarily quantitative.

Vital Depression

Somewhat reminiscent of Pollitt's *S* type of depression is the concept of *vital depressions,* which has played an important role in the classification of depression in Europe. Van Praag (1965) characterized vital depression in the following way: it occurs without apparent reason, is motiveless, incomprehensible, and apparently senseless. He contrasts it with the "personal depressions," which are congruous with the environmental situation and in which the primary symptoms are in the emotional sphere. In contrast, vital depressives will have, in addition to the emotional feelings of depression, symptoms of retardation with a generalized slowing down in intellectual and physical capacity; difficulties in thinking; feelings of indifference; decreased emotional receptivity; and typically loss of appetite, difficulty with sleep, and an overwhelming sense of fatigue. Finally, Van Praag suggested that spontaneous fluctuation of the patient's clinical state, with symptoms being appreciably worse before noon, is characteristic of the vital syndrome. Historically, European diagnosticians regarded vital depression as the "cardinal symptom of all endogenous depressions" (Schneider, 1920). However, Van Praag and contemporary European researchers reject this association, saying that there is no evidence to associate this constellation of symptoms with the concept of etiology implied in the term endogenous depression (see page 44 for further discussion). Thus the term vital syndrome or vital depression is used strictly as a descriptive concept.

Bipolar/Unipolar Depressions

Perris (1966) suggested that a meaningful distinction can be made between *bipolar* and *unipolar recurrent depressive illness:* bipolar recurrent depression is used to describe people who have had both depressive and manic episodes (manic-depressive illness); unipolar depression refers to people who have had several depressive episodes but who have never been manic. Table 2 summarizes the findings from a study in which he com-

TABLE 2: Characteristics of Bipolar and Unipolar Depressions (Adapted from Perris, 1966)

Variable	Bipolar Depression	Unipolar Depression
Genetic investigation	If two members of one family become depressed, then it is probable that both will develop either a bipolar or a unipolar illness (see also Chapter Nine).	
Childhood environment	No significant differences concerning childhood bereavement between the two groups. Higher incidence of unfavorable home conditions in the bipolar group.	
Precipitating factors	No significant differences between the groups. Tendency to more frequent somatic factors among unipolars.	
Celibacy	Significantly higher number of celibates among male bipolar patients than male unipolars. No difference concerning women.	
Fertility	No significant differences between the groups.	
Personality traits	Significant predominance of syntonic personality pattern.	Significant predominance of asthenic personality pattern.
Median age at onset	About 30 years.	About 45 years.
Body build	No significant differences between the groups.	
Color-form preference	More pronounced color preference during both depressive phase and remission.	More pronounced color preference during depressive phase.
Flicker threshold	Lower than controls both during depressive phase and remission.	Somewhat low during depressive phase. Higher than in bipolar patients.
Clinical rating	No significant differences either in anxiety-depression or in retardation scores.	
Response to treatment	Require fewer ECT.	Require more ECT.
Course	Somewhat shorter episodes, more frequent relapses.	Somewhat longer episodes, less frequent relapses.
Suicide	No significant differences between the groups.	

pared two such groups of depressed patients. It can be seen from this table that there are a number of significant differences between the two groups. Perris suggested that the differences cannot be explained on the basis of severity of the illness alone and believed that the two kinds of depression were two different illnesses.

Factor-Analytic Studies

A number of studies have attempted to classify depression through the use of factor-analytic techniques. Factor analysis is a statistical method of discovering and explaining correlations between variables. It aims at identifying the smallest number of factors (groups of items) that will account for the bulk of the variance in a given set of data. These factors provide alternative ways of understanding the relationship of these items to each other. The relationship is expressed in terms of a *loading* or score for each item. Loadings can vary from +1.00 to −1.00. A high loading (plus or minus) indicates that an item is closely associated with the factor and a loading near zero indicates little relationship. A plus loading means a direct relationship between factor and item; a negative loading means an inverse relationship.

There have been a number of factor-analytic studies of depression; that conducted by Grinker and his associates (1961) is one of the most careful and detailed. Checklists recording feelings, concerns, and current behavior were completed for a group of depressed patients under carefully controlled conditions. After a series of statistical analyses there were four patterns of symptomatology that accounted for most of the patients studied. These clinical profiles are summarized in Table 3.

As shown in the table, type A patients had feelings of helplessness and low self-esteem; some guilt; isolation and withdrawal; apathy; slowing of speech and thought; and a more favorable response to somatic therapy than to psychotherapy. Furthermore, factor pattern A types were not hypochondriacal, clinging, or demanding, and there were only a few somatic symptoms. Grinker et al. regarded this type as an "empty" person who has "given up," and suggested that the pattern is close to the common stereotype of depression. It also bears some resemblance to the endogenous factor mentioned later in this chapter.

Type B patients had feelings commonly associated with depression but were particularly marked by the presence of a considerable amount of anxiety. One of the interesting observations to emerge from this study was that the diagnosis of depression by clinicians to a large extent is determined not only by the presence of a depressed mood but also by the pres-

TABLE 3: Four Factor Patterns of Depressive Syndromes[a]

	Type A ("Empty")	Type B ("Anxious")	Type C ("Hypochondriacal")	Type D ("Angry")
Feelings	Dismal, hopeless, low self-esteem, guilt	Dismal, hopeless, low self-esteem, anxiety	Deprivation of love	Gloomy, hopeless, guilt, anxiety
Behavior	Withdrawn, apathetic, retarded	Agitation, clinging, demands for attention	Agitation, demanding, hypochondriacal, psychosomatic symptoms	Demanding, provocative
Treatment response	Poor to psychotherapy better to somatic therapy	Often good to psychotherapy and tranquilizers	Poor to ECT, better to pharmacological therapy and supportive psychotherapy	Poor to psychotherapy because of danger of "rage suicide"; somatic therapy often required

[a]Grinker, R. R., et al. *The Phenomenon of Depression* (New York: Paul B. Holber, 1961); as adapted by Lehmann, H. E., *Pharmacotherapy of Depression*. Cole, J. O. and Wittenborn, J. R. Eds. (Springfield: Charles C. Thomas, 1966).

ence of anxiety. In fact, Grinker, et al. found that patients were diagnosed as depressed, even if they were only mildly sad, if there was a considerable amount of anxiety present.

Type C patients did not complain of severe feelings of depression, but instead complained of persistent and exaggerated physical complaints. They were markedly irrational and demanding in their hypochondriasis.

Type D patients were somewhat similar to the B type, with a considerable amount of gloom, hopelessness, and anxiety. However, they were not as withdrawn as the B patients. They showed anger and tried to control their environment through their illness by manipulating friends and family; this control was achieved by imposing their helplessness on others and by provoking feelings of pity and guilt in others.

Other Studies. Of the many other factor-analytic studies that have been conducted, there are seven in which factors suitable for comparison

TABLE 4: Factor Loadings of Unrotated Endogenous Factors from Various Studies

Study	K&G[a]	R&K[b]	H&W[c]	R&G[d]	M&C[e]	CR&G[f]	H
Personal details							
Age	25	31 *	X	ns *	45	21	X
Personality traits							
Obsessionality	−20	ns *	X	25 *	62	X	X
Hysterical features (immaturity)	−41	−28 *	X	ns *	−53	X	X
Inadequacy	−32	ns *	X	X	−66	−39	X
Previous history							
Previous attacks of depression	23	X	X	23 *	00	49	X

Key

  *—Items not included in factor analysis but later correlated with factor.

  ns—Correlation not reported but described as "not significant."

  ±—Item (or factor) reflected to agree with direction of scoring or loadings in other studies.

  X—Item not included in study.

Authors and Characteristics of Samples

  [a] K&G—Kiloh and Garside (1963), 102 male and 41 female outpatients.

  [b] R&K—Rosenthal and Klerman (1966), charts of 50 female inpatients.

  [c] H&W—Hamilton and White (1959), 49 male inpatients.

  [d] R&G—Rosenthal and Gudeman (1967), 50 female inpatients and 50 female outpatients.

  [e] M&C—Mendels and Cochrane (1970, in preparation), 100 male and female inpatients.

  [f] CR&G—Carney, Roth, and Garside (1965), 120 inpatients, sex not mentioned.

  [g] Ho—Hordern (1965), 137 female inpatients.

Study	K&G	R&K	H&W	R&G	M&C	CR&G	Ho
Present illness							
Precipitants	−48	−29 *	X	−23 *	−40	−35	X
Depth of depression	37	65	76	53	X	X	75
Reactivity of							
depression	−60	−26	X	−67	X	−57	X
Depression worse							
in morning	53	08	X	12	X	06	X
in evening	−17	−13	X	31	16	−28	X
Self reproach or guilt	20	50	73	54	13	67	70
Retardation	55	55	68	57	48	X	47
Agitation (motor							
restlessness)	17	44	−03	53	−49	X	60
Weight loss (7 lb.							
or more)	32	45	35	25	10	36	25
Irritability	−17	−20	X	−04	X	−47	X
Hypochondriasis	−12	10	16	06	−12	−62	26
Self-pity	−32	−22	X	−31	X	−55	X
Variability of illness	−39	04	X	29	−28	−57	X
Initial insomnia	−24	37	21	26	07	−31	33
Middle insomnia	X	70	28	52	X	X	31
Early awakening	69	59	34	42	−01	23	22
Visceral symptoms	X	44	28	53	X	X	36
Loss of interest	X	42	46	51	X	X	65
Suicide							
ideas	13	X	X	X	−17	X	X
attempts	23	X	X	X	−30	X	X
ideas and/or							
attempts	X	10	53	43	X	22	48
Anxiety							
psychic	−08	X	−37	37	X	X	65
somatic	X	X	−40	23	X	X	44
psychic and/							
or somatic	X	17	X	X	X	−69	X

have been reported. All seven studies were primarily concerned with the division of depressed patients into endogenous and reactive groups. Table 4 presents a comparison of findings by Hamilton and White (1959); Kiloh and Garside (1963); Carney, Roth, and Garside (1965); Hordern (1965); Rosenthal and Klerman (1966); Rosenthal and Gudeman (1967); and Mendels and Cochrane (in preparation).

In order to determine the amount of agreement between these seven studies, 25 historical, personality, or symptom items were compared between studies (Mendels and Cochrane, 1968). For purposes of this analysis, two studies were said to agree on an item if *both* showed either significant plus loadings, significant minus loadings, or no significant loadings for that particular item. Since factor loadings can be interpreted as correlations, statistical significance was determined by what size correlation was needed for a 0.05 probability level (that is, the chances are better than 95 out of a 100 that a finding is significant and not coincidental).

For the purpose of this comparison, Mendels and Cochrane used the following definitions:

1. *Perfect Agreement.* All studies agreed on the direction and significance of a given item's loadings; that is, studies that included this item found it to be significantly associated with the same factor. Eight items met this criterion. The directions of the loadings were such that a patient described as an endogenous depressive was characterized as being retarded, deeply depressed, lacking in reactivity to environmental changes, showing a loss of interest in life, having bodily symptoms, lacking a precipitating stress, having middle-of-the-night insomnia, and not showing self-pity.

2. *Fair Agreement.* At least 75 percent of the studies agreed on the direction and significance of the loadings of an item, and the studies that did not agree were only minimally contradictory; that is, they did not yield a significant loading in the opposite direction.

Nine items were judged as showing fair agreement. They describe the endogenous depressive as being older, having a history of previous episodes, showing weight loss, having early-morning awakening, showing self-reproach or guilt, and not showing personality features suggesting hysteria or inadequacy. Suicidal thoughts, threats, or attempts also characterized the "endogenous" factor. Contrary to classical thinking, diurnal variation of symptoms did not relate to this factor.

Two other items, which showed perfect agreement in three studies, should be noted: perception of the depression as qualitatively different from ordinary sadness or downcast spirits, and the absence of hysterical symptoms. Both were part of the endogenous factor.

3. Disagreement. Items showed markedly different relationships to the

"endogenous" factor in different studies. These included obsessional personality, depression worse in the evening, agitation, hypochondriasis, variability of illness, anxiety, and initial insomnia. There are several possible explanations for the disagreement between studies on these items. The terms may mean different things to different raters; if "different" variables are given the same name, there is of course no reason why results should be the same. The factor-analytic results may also be distorted if the variables are differentially related to sex. For example, agitation and initial insomnia show clear positive loadings in the studies using only females but not in those using males or both sexes.

Assessment. Underlying these problems is the possibility that the theoretical framework of the investigators might have influenced the findings. This framework would have influenced not only the ways in which information was obtained (for example, how the questions were asked) but also the perceptions of the investigators in terms of which patient responses were encouraged or emphasized and which were minimized. Such responses may be very subtle; a frown, an inflection in the voice, a murmur of encouragement, will all influence the patient's reactions and provide him with cues as to the answers he thinks the investigator would like to have. This desire to provide the right answers and to please the investigator is widespread and will influence the information obtained.

In addition to influencing patient responses, the investigator's theoretical concepts may affect his results. An investigator who accepts the validity of the endogenous-reactive dichotomy may, on learning that a patient is complaining of early-morning wakening, assume (unconsciously perhaps) that the patient probably has endogenous depression. This assumption will, of course, influence him and the data he collects.

In spite of these problems the Mendels and Cochrane review reveals an impressive amount of agreement between factor-analytic studies. This agreement is even more impressive in view of the diversity of patient populations (age, sex, country), and the training and theoretical conceptions of the investigators.

Although there is considerable agreement in these studies that certain items tend to cluster and form discrete factors, there is a difference of opinion about the significance of the factors. The factor reviewed above is often regarded as representing "endogenous" depression. As has been indicated, the term "endogenous" has specific etiological implications. However, there is only limited evidence from the factor-analytic studies to support these implications.

Interpretations other than the etiological one can be made. For example, the question must be considered of whether the factor is measuring *severity* or simply a pure or *classic depression* picture. Many patients who fit textbook descriptions in some regard also show additional features, supposedly characteristic of other disorders. The factor under discussion may indicate that in a large group of patients with depression there are a number who demonstrate a fairly pure depressive picture, and that in others there are features of hysteria, character disorder (inadequacy), anxiety, and other nondepressive characteristics. Thus the so-called endogenous factor may represent the core of depressive symptomatology, whereas the clinical features of the reactive factor may represent symptoms of psychiatric disorders other than depression, which, when present, contaminate the depression syndrome. When depression is present in association with these other features, it might be regarded as just one of several symptoms, any one of which might dominate.

CHAPTER FIVE

PSYCHOLOGICAL THEORIES

There are a number of psychological theories that advance explanations about the causes of pathological depression. We shall consider these theories in two groups: those that suggest that depression (and mania) is primarily a mood disturbance—an *affective* disorder; and one that suggests that depression is primarily a *cognitive* disorder—a disturbance in thought processes. We shall review some of the experimental work that has been done in an effort to provide validation for these theories, and then note some general criticisms and an overall evaluation of some of the more important features of the psychological theories.

AFFECTIVE PSYCHOLOGICAL THEORIES

Abraham and Freud (Psychoanalytic Theories)

In 1911 Abraham made the first systematic attempt to explain manic-depressive illness in terms of psychoanalytic theory by comparing depression with normal grief or mourning. He suggested that the crucial difference between grief and depression is that a mourner is consciously concerned with the lost person, but a depressed patient is dominated by his feelings of loss, guilt, and low self-esteem. For the depressed patient, unconscious feelings of hostility toward the lost person (either real or symbolic) are directed toward himself, as are the deficiencies and weaknesses he had attributed (usually unconsciously) to the lost person. Abraham suggested the depressive perceives a loss as rejection of himself because of the way in which he unconsciously confuses it with earlier traumatic and sensitizing experiences.

In his 1917 paper *Mourning and Melancholia* Freud expanded Abraham's ideas to provide a theoretical basis for depression in terms of psychoanalytic theory. According to Freud, the essential difference between grief and depression was that in the latter there was a marked loss of self-esteem. Thus, he wrote, "in grief the world becomes poor and empty; in melancholia it is the ego itself." Also, in mourning the loss is conscious, whereas in depression the true loss is unconscious.

Freud suggested that in the normal course of mourning the mourner withdraws the emotions previously associated with the lost person, and himself becomes identified with these feelings. His previously unexpressed and perhaps unrecognized ambivalent feelings of hatred to the lost object are turned onto himself. This is characterized by:

1. Anger directed toward the lost object, arising from feelings of resentment and desertion.

2. Feelings of guilt, stemming from the mourner's real or imagined sins of omission (or commission), toward the lost object.

3. A self-centered sense of suffering and loss.

Freud suggested that it is necessary to resolve these feelings by grief or mourning "work," which involves the conscious recall and expression of memories and fantasies. Each time this is done, there is a gradual loosening of the bonds that tied the mourner to the lost person. This reduction of ties allows a gradual redirection of emotions toward new tasks and relationships.

It is, of course, apparent that the loss of a love object, regarded by Freud as essential in the development of depression, need not involve the actual death of a person. He suggested that the withdrawal of love and support by a significant figure (usually a parent) during a crucial stage of development predisposes an individual to depression later in life. According to Freud, it is this loss, later recapitulated in symbolic form, that gives rise to the depression. Depression, then, could be seen as a failure of the normal mourning process.

Freud suggested that a depressed patient has also suffered a loss, although it may be symbolic and not recognized as loss. He considered the self-reproach and the loss of self-esteem that develop in depression as being directed toward the introjected and lost person; that is, when a depressed patient dwells on his own misdemeanors, deficiencies, and inadequacies, he is expressing his unconscious feelings about the lost person.

Instead of simply identifying with the lost person, the patient assumes the perceived attributes of this person; as a result he relates exaggerated accounts of his own sins and inadequacies, even though they have no relationship in reality to his own life; they represent his concepts and unexpressed feelings about the object. Freud described it in this way:

> An object-choice, an attachment of the libido to a particular person, had at one time existed; then owing to a real slight or disappointment coming from this loved person, the object-relationship was shattered. The result was not the normal one of a withdrawal of the libido from this object and a displacement of it onto a new one, but something different for whose coming about various conditions seem to be necessary. The object-cathexis proved to have little power of resistance and was brought to an end. But the free libido was not displaced onto another object; it was withdrawn into the ego. There, however, it was not employed in any unspecified way, but served to establish an identification of the ego with the abandoned object. Thus, the shadow of the object fell upon the ego, and the latter could henceforth be judged by a special agency, as though it were an object, a forsaken object. In this way an object loss was transformed into an ego loss and the conflict between the ego and the lost person into a cleavage between the critical activity of the ego and the ego as altered by identification (Freud, 1917).

Thus the depression becomes a narcissistic inner-directed process, instead of being outer-directed. A marked feature of the symptomatology of a depressed patient is its sadomasochistic character. This arises from ambivalence toward the incorporated lost object and causes the patient to express ideas of self-abuse and self-denigration and frequently leads to self-destructive behavior. Freud also emphasized a marked oral dependency (an exaggerated need for continuous emotional support) in depressed patients.

Abraham developed Freud's theoretical postulates further and suggested that there are several difficulties in childhood development that provide the basis for the emergence of a depressive illness later in life. These include the occurrence of significant emotional difficulties during the oral phase of infantile development (before resolution of the oedipal complex). The source of these difficulties is usually withdrawal of love from the infant. According to Abraham this results in a fixation of emotional development at the oral stage, with a consequent exaggeration of *oral eroticism,* which involves not only a marked dependency on sources of direct oral satisfaction but also a general dependency on people and events to supply emotional gratification. According to this theory there is a recapitulation (symbolic) of the primary infantile loss later in life, leading to a depressive reaction.

Klein

Melanie Klein (1948) proposed a different psychodynamic basis for the development of depression. According to Klein, the basis for depression is formed during the first year of life. She suggested that all infants normally pass through a developmental stage, which she termed the *depressive position*—a phase of sadness, fear, and guilt. The infant feels frustrated by a lack of love (its demands are impossible to meet at this time) and becomes angry at the mother, developing destructive and sadistic fantasies toward her. The infant comes to fear that these fantasies will actually destroy the mother and develops feelings of anxiety and guilt. Furthermore, the infant is unable to differentiate between the external world (the mother) and the internal world (itself and its internal images of the mother), and the fear of destroying the mother becomes, in part, a fear of destroying itself. This is the phase that Klein termed the depressive position.

Normally the infant realizes that the mother he hates (the *bad object*) and the mother he loves (the *good object*) are actually one (a *whole object*). This leads to a satisfactory resolution of the depressive position. However, if there is a failure to bring these two together (a failure to establish a *good internal object*) because the feelings of aggression and hatred are stronger than the feelings of love, the pathological basis is set for the development of depressions in adult life.

Many workers have taken exception to Klein's application of adult reactions, values, and emotions to the infant's psyche. Further, no evidence is available about the relationship between the occurrence of depression in adult life and the occurrence of clinical depression in childhood, which was described by such workers as Spitz (1946).

Bibring

Edward Bibring (1953) emphasized a loss of self-esteem as the crucial element in depression. His views contrasted with those of the earlier psychoanalytic theorists in that he placed more emphasis on ego psychology (conscious response to events) than on unconscious conflicts between ego and superego. Although he agreed with the earlier psychoanalytic workers on the importance of initial childhood experiences in predisposing adults toward the development of depression, he suggested that clinical depression develops primarily as a consequence of frustration of conscious expectations. Thus he wrote, "The emotional expression of a state of helplessness and powerlessness of the ego, irrespective of what may have caused the breakdown of the mechanisms which establish the self esteem, constitutes the essence of the condition." He also differed from the earlier psychoanalysts in regard to their belief that difficulties in handling aggressive feelings played a crucial role in the genesis of depression.

Benedek

Therese Benedek (1956) stressed the importance of the *depressive constellation,* a term used to describe a psychological state arising from difficulties in the early mother-child relationship. A child, satisfied by the oral experience and satisfaction of feeding, will introject a concept of *the good feeding mother* and equate this with the *good satiated self.* Ideally, this should set up a cycle in which mother and child both gain increasing self-confidence and promote confidence and gratification in each other.

However, when an infant is not gratified he will become extremely aggressive. When eating he introjects this aggressive impulse and thus, instead of the equation good feeding mother is good satiated self, there develops a state of *bad mother equals bad self.* Benedek suggests that this constitutes a basis for depression in later life, when appropriate stresses cause regression to this oral phase.

Arieti

Arieti (1959) postulated another theory of the development of manic-depressive illness. Initially a baby is well cared for by an accepting and providing mother. The infant responds by developing a willingness to accept everything that he is offered; he is receptive to his mother's influence. This leads to the development of a personality characterized by features of extroversion, conformity, acceptance of surrounding value systems, and a degree of dependence. Arieti suggested that this *psychological receptivity* also predisposes the child to exaggerated introjection.

At some time toward the end of the first year or during the second year of life the typical mother of a potential manic-depressive changes significantly in her behavior toward the child. While continuing to attend to his needs, she becomes less generous with her time and emotions and begins making demands on him. When this change is associated with the parents' dissatisfaction and resentment at their life situation, or with the increased responsibility represented by their children, the resentment and aggression is not expressed directly but is manifested as an increase in expectations from the child. Thus "the child will receive care and affection provided he accepts the expectations that the parents have for him and tries to live up to them."

Frequently, Arieti suggested, this change in attitude by the parents (especially the mother) is associated with or even precipitated by the arrival of a new baby in the home. The child's response is to attempt to meet the parents' expectations, no matter what cost and strain are involved. "It is only by complying, obeying, and working hard that he will recapture the love or state of bliss which he used to have as a baby, or at least maintain that moderate love which he is receiving now." The child now feels that the love of a parent is conditioned by his own giving to them. The flow of love is intermittent and, as a consequence, his security is decreasing. Considerable anxiety results from the fear that his failures to comply and live up to his mother's expectations may lead to the total withdrawal of her love as a form of punishment. The child comes to feel that whether the parent loves him is entirely in his own hands: it is dependent on whether he earns it. He sees rejection and punishment as efforts by the mother to help him to be good and deserving of her love. The punishment is now seen as good, a method whereby he can achieve a behavior pattern that will warrant her love. Believing, then, that the absence of parental love is his responsibility, he feels guilty, a feeling that leads to the development of a need for still more punishment in the hope that punishment will absolve the guilt and return him to his mother's favor.

Arieti pointed to two other mechanisms that he regards as important in the genesis of the manic-depressive state. The developmental pattern described above leads to rage, resentment and feelings of violent aggression toward the parents. However, this is usually brought under rigid control and rarely acted out. It does give rise to additional guilt feelings, with associated feelings of unworthiness and depression.

Finally, Arieti suggested that the child tends to internalize other significant adults in the environment. However, this usually fails and "may end by confusing the child (how can he satisfy all the adults?) and increasing his burdens of guilt."

SYSTEMATIC STUDIES OF PSYCHODYNAMIC THEORIES

Family and Personality Studies

Among the few attempts that have been made by psychoanalysts to examine some of their theories systematically is that of Mabel Blake Cohen et al. (1954), who studied the family background, patterns of interpersonal relationships, and personality characteristics of 12 patients with a diagnosis of manic-depressive psychosis.

The authors concluded that all 12 patients came from a family background that was marked in some way by feelings of social inferiority or undesirability; the families were characterized by belonging to a racial minority, having suffered recent financial reverses, or having a member of the immediate family with a history of mental illness. They had a markedly upward-striving pattern of behavior and usually placed the primary responsibility for this "uplifting" of the family on one child. The authors suggest—perhaps too inconclusively—that this child, selected for such reasons as being the youngest, the oldest, the most intelligent, or perhaps the only child in the family, was subjected to considerable pressure to surpass his peers, and the family derived considerable satisfaction from his achievements. This intensely competitive situation for the child was interpreted by him as being "his responsibility" toward his family. This was the child who later developed manic-depressive illness.

The typical mother of these manic-depressive patients was described by the authors as the strongest member of the family, the one who exercised discipline and who transmitted demands to the child. She also tended to deprecate the father, portraying him as weak and ineffectual. As a consequence, the child developed considerable ambivalence in his feelings toward the mother, with dislike and aggression often dominating.

During childhood, adolescence, and young adult life the potential manic-depressive was often an apparently well-adjusted, conforming, striving, and overconscientious individual whose most conspicuous characteristics were his drive to achieve and the problems he experienced if he failed to achieve a particular goal. There was a denial of the ambivalent feelings toward his parents, a repression of the aggressive and rebellious drive, and an apparent indifference to emotional needs and feelings in himself or in others. He seemed to operate on an all-or-nothing basis; things were either good, desirable, and acceptable or bad and rejected. He had difficulty in perceiving the shadings of human personality and behavior. Cohen et al. suggested that this reflects the child's difficulty in adequately accepting the various, often contradictory, facets of his parents' relationship with him.

Psychotic episodes were precipitated in these patients by real or symbolic rejection or by failure to achieve set goals. In these episodes patients regressed to an earlier stage in which, according to Cohen, failure to achieve the high standards set by the parents had led to rejection by the mother and consequent feelings of guilt for having let her and the family down.

Although the Cohen et al. study was careful and thorough, it was based on a very small number of patients and the authors left unanswered a number of important questions. For example, why do only a small percentage of people who come from a family environment described as characteristic of the manic depressive in fact develop this illness? The majority, of course, do not. It is apparent to the most casual observer that such factors as belonging to a minority group, having a dominating mother and a weak father, coming from a family that has suffered financial reverses, and being subjected to excessive demands in childhood are widespread, and in themselves cannot account for the occurrence in later life of manic-depressive psychosis.

Gibson (1957) attempted to validate the findings of Cohen's group. He compared the original 12 manic-depressive patients studied by Cohen et al. with a group of 27 manic-depressive patients and 17 schizophrenic patients. He devised a questionnaire to record the characteristics of the family and personality that Cohen had suggested as important, and data were obtained by trained social workers. Gibson claimed that this study confirmed that the two groups of manic-depressive patients could be differentiated from the schizophrenic patients by three characteristics:

1. The manic-depressive family showed a greater degree of striving for prestige and had selected the patient as the instrument for this need.
2. The childhood background of the manic-depressive patient was characterized by competitiveness and envy.
3. There was a marked concern about social achievement and social improvement in the family of the manic-depressive patient.

In addition to such limitations in this study as failure to control adequately for age and the unreliability of data collection, there is a problem in determining if the family background of manic-depressive patients differs in a significant manner from that of other psychiatric patients and from control subjects; the fact that they differed from a group of schizophrenics may reflect some characteristics of the schizophrenic group rather than of the manic-depressive group. And, again, why is it that only a small minority of people with this particular kind of background develop this illness when the majority seem either to escape without significant psychiatric impairment or to develop other forms of psychiatric disorder?

Becker et al. conducted a series of studies to further explore the hypotheses proposed by Cohen et al. They studied the personality characteristics of manic-depressive patients in an attempt to determine whether there were observable manifestations of excessive parental demands for conformity and achievement. In an initial comparison (Becker, 1960) of manic depressives with nonpsychiatric controls, it was found that the manic-depressive subjects differed significantly in personality from the controls. The manic depressives were characterized by an excess of conventional attitudes and traditional opinions and achievement concepts. However, in a later study Becker et al. (1963) compared patients diagnosed as manic depressive with patients diagnosed as neurotic depressive or schizophrenic and with a group of normal controls. This time they could find no significant differences in personality characteristics of conventionality, achievement drives, and so forth among the three groups of psychiatric patients. All three groups of psychiatric patients differed significantly from the normal control subjects. This, of course, strongly suggested that the background and personality characteristics ascribed by Cohen et al. to the manic depressive may, in fact, simply have been a background basis for the experience of psychiatric illness in general.

Depression in Infants

Anaclitic Depression. Spitz (1946) described a syndrome of severe depression occurring in some hospitalized infants; he termed it *anaclitic depression.* This syndrome developed after an abrupt separation from a mother who had previously been responsive to an infant's needs; the mother was replaced by an unfamiliar, often impersonal figure. After an initial period of distress manifested by crying, screaming, protesting, and looking around, the children became depressed. They were apathetic, unresponsive, cried silently if at all, and looked very sad. There was little interest in people, in food, or in toys. If reunited with their mothers, they usually showed a significant improvement in their mood and behavior, although there occasionally was an interim period of unresponsiveness to the mother. This period was usually followed by a protracted period during which the child manifested a marked overdependency on its mother, with severe frustration at any separation and a considerable fear of strangers and removal from familiar environments.

Depression-Withdrawal. Engel (1962) described a very similar reaction in a single child, Monica, whose mother was unable to handle her with warmth and affection because of the child's physical abnormalities. Monica had a congenital abnormality of the esophagus that made swallowing impossible. Consequently, she had to be fed through a gastric fistula, a tube leading from the stomach through to the external abdominal wall. At the age of 15 months Monica weighed only 10 pounds and was very depressed. Her low weight was not from poor food intake; in spite of her physical abnormalities she received an adequate caloric provision. Engel suggested that Monica's poor relationship with her mother and consequent depression was the basis for her physical and mental retardation. In the hospital the staff established an intensive relationship with her. After several months she showed a marked improvement and resumed normal development. However, she continued to suffer transient depressions.

Engel described Monica's responses as *depression-withdrawal.* He suggested that when the initial distress and crying of an infant fail to produce relief—that is, to produce the good satisfying mother—the child is faced with an overwhelming anxiety and a consequent exhaustion. He depicted depression-withdrawal as a defense mechanism involving regression to a stage of development prior to the formation of identification with specific environmental objects, especially the mother. There is an extreme degree of withdrawal, both emotional and physical. An inability to respond appropriately to people is accompanied by a withdrawal from food and a reduction in oral behavior and gastric secretions. The child thus avoids the frustration of continuous crying; effects "both a massive withdrawal from contact with the unsatisfying environment and a reduction of activity in the interest of conservation of energy" (1962). Engel suggested that this is a primitive, last-ditch effort at self-preservation, and that emotional states of helplessness and hopelessness will later evolve from it.

Helplessness and *hopelessness* have been described by Schmale (1958, 1962) as the emotional states that occur in man when he feels that "it is the end." *Helplessness* is the term applied when the individual gives up because of a failure of external sources of emotional support. He does not feel responsible for his dilemma or capable of influencing it. *Hopelessness* is a state that occurs when he feels personally responsible for the situation and believes that nothing he or anyone else can do will alter it. He also has feelings of worthlessness, believing that he does not deserve assistance from others. Adult helplessness has as its analogue in infancy the initial reaction of intense anxiety felt by a baby who has been separated from its parents; adult hopelessness has as its analogue in infancy the state of depression-withdrawal.

Animal Studies

Experimental studies of the effects of separation of baby monkeys from their mothers provide some indirect support for the hypotheses discussed in the preceding section.

Kaufman and Rosenblum (1967) found that three out of four baby monkeys reacted to separation from their mothers by an initial period of agitated searching, followed by an apparently deeply depressed phase. They compared this biphasic response in the infant monkeys with Engel's observations: the initial removal of the mother produced in the infant monkey a distress reaction "characterized by a high level of motoric, visceral-autonomic, vocal and expressive activity, which ordinarily functions to regain mother's comfort-producing stimuli." They assumed that this was associated with the emotion of *apprehension* (precursor of anxiety). However, the mother is not there to respond and persistence of the stress gives rise to the next phase: *conservation-withdrawal* (depression-withdrawal). In this phase the infant monkeys show a "postural collapse, immobility, withdrawal from the environment, and reduction in visceral-autonomic, vocal and expressive activity." This was assumed by Kaufman and Rosenblum to be associated with the unpleasant feeling of *pessimism* (the precursor of depression). They suggested that this was a conservation reaction designed to preserve a degree of stability in the organism until comfort-producing stimuli reappeared.

It is of interest to note that after about a week of this abnormal behavior, spontaneous recovery seemed to occur in the infant monkeys, even though the mothers did not return. Later when they were returned to their mothers there was an increase in physical contact between infant and mother and a decrease in play and relationship with peers. The infants stayed closer to their mothers, and when they did move away it was for shorter periods of time than previously. The authors concluded that the mother-infant relationship had become much closer as a result of the separation.

General Criticisms

Mendelson (1960) reviewed in detail the psychoanalytic literature on depression. He criticized psychoanalysts for concentrating most of their efforts on abstract theoretical models, with little or no emphasis on critical scientific investigation. He described the literature as a "not-so-great monolog," a "great debate" instead of a "great investigation," and suggested that the theoretical models postulated had little relevant relationship to clinical reality. Further, he thought that a self-perpetuating cycle had been established, in which there was a general tendency to accept these models uncritically and to apply them to individual patients, rather than critically inquiring whether the dynamics of the individual patient supported or refuted the theoretical concept.

Grinker et al. (1961) have also stated this problem:

> From these theoretical psychoanalytic discussions, there has developed a stereotype of the psychodynamics of depression which is unrelated to the variations in the clinical picture. It is this stereotype which has influenced psychiatrists today to assume that, once given a symptomatology of depression, the formulation of the psychodynamics can be reeled off with facile fluency. These basic formulations, stereotype though they may be and agreed upon as they are by so many, have never been validated and despite their universal acceptance by many authors, they are far from applicable to individual cases or groups of cases.

COGNITIVE PSYCHOLOGICAL THEORIES

It is generally considered that the thought disorder that depressed patients manifest is a consequence of a basic disturbance in mood. However, Beck (1967) has suggested that it is a primary disturbance in thinking that causes the development of the disturbed mood state. "The affective response is determined by the way an individual structures his experience. Thus, if an individual's conceptualization of a situation has an unpleasant content he will experience a corresponding unpleasant affective response."

Beck proposed that each person has a *schema*—a pattern or framework of thought—with which he approaches and experiences life; the nature and specific characteristics of this schema determine individual responses. For example, he suggested that people who develop depression have schemas concerned with self-deprecation; those who develop anxiety states have schemas concerned with the anticipation of personal harm, and so forth.

It is an observable clinical fact that depressed patients have abnormal thinking patterns. When a patient says that he is worthless, useless, or bad; that his bowels are blocked up; that he has some incurable disease; that the law is after him; or that he is rejected and reviled by his friends and family, he is usually not stating the truth. In addition to these examples of distortion of reality, depressed patients frequently manifest many milder forms of disordered thinking, such as unwarranted pessimism or fear of rejection. It is a fact that it is usually not possible to talk the patient out of these views. His thinking remains fixed and the development of the pattern usually parallels the course of the illness.

Beck has attempted to analyze the primary characteristics of thinking in depressed patients as compared with nondepressed psychiatric patients. Based on data derived primarily from observations made during psychotherapeutic interviews, he suggested that there are important differences, and that "each nosological group showed an idiosyncratic ideational content that distinguished it from each of the others."

Among the thinking patterns Beck regards as characteristic of depressed patients are: low self-regard, ideas of deprivation, self-criticism and self-blame, exaggerated ideas of duty and responsibilities, frequent self-commands and injunctions, and escapist and suicidal wishes. Underlying all these is a distortion of reality, and a systematic bias by the patients against themselves. The following are the thought processes that Beck (1967) regarded as important in the development of this cognitive state.

1. *Arbitrary inference,* which is a tendency to draw a conclusion (usually of a personally denigratory nature) from a situation that is essentially neutral or impersonal. For example a woman may feel uncomfortable when shopping because she thinks the sales clerks think poorly of her; there is no factual basis for this idea. There is a failure to realize that there are more probable explanations for particular situations.

2. *Selected abstraction,* a concentration on one aspect of a situation that is taken out of context and exaggerated. This occurs when an individual, corrected for one minor aspect of his work, immediately jumps to the conclusion that everything he does is inadequate; he cannot be easily dissuaded from this idea.

3. *Overgeneralization,* which involves an overall conclusion based on a

single, often minor, experience or incident. Beck cited the example of a patient who reported the following sequence of events: "His wife was upset because the children were slow in getting dressed. He thought, 'I am a poor father because the children are not better disciplined.' He then noticed a leaky faucet, and thought that this showed he was also a poor husband. While driving to work, he thought, 'I must be a poor driver or other cars would not be passing me.' As he arrived at work, he noticed some other personnel had already arrived. He thought, 'I can't be very dedicated or I would have come earlier.' When he noticed folders and papers piled up on his desk, he concluded 'I am a poor organizer because I have so much work to do" (Beck, 1967).

4. *Magnification and minimization,* distorted evaluations and exaggerations of a situation or experience. Here a person exaggerates his difficulties and limitations and minimizes his achievements and capacities.

5. *Inexact labeling,* the labeling of an experience in an exaggerated fashion, with a consequent direct association between the affective response and the label instead of between the actual response and the actual experience. Thus the emotional response to a situation relates more to the way in which it is labeled or described than to the actual event. This is an extension of magnification.

On the basis of these and other observations, Beck suggests that it would be appropriate to consider depression as a "primary disorder of thought with a resultant disturbance of affect and behavior in consonance with the cognitive distortion," rather than a primary affective disturbance.

However, to validate Beck's hypothesis that this thought disturbance is primary, it is necessary to demonstrate that the thought processes of depressed patients are in fact different both from normal subjects and other groups of psychiatric patients. It will also be necessary to demonstrate that the cognitive disturbance is primary and not consequent on the development of an affective disturbance.

OVERALL EVALUATION

Several features have been repeatedly stressed as characterizing either the premorbid personality of patients who develop depression or the depressive process itself. These include the experience of loss; feelings of guilt; feelings of aggression, and oral dependent needs. All these features have been referred to in this discussion of psychological theories. Since they occupy so central a place in these theories (and by implication in the psychotherapy) of depression, a closer look at their relationship with depression is warranted.

Guilt

Guilt is regarded by many theoreticians as the central component of depression, and a large number of depressed patients do express strong feelings of guilt that have no basis in reality. However, the universality of this association must be questioned. Many depressed patients are not burdened with guilt feelings, and even those who are seem to develop them in a secondary, almost incidental, manner.

Recent observations about college students, for example, have suggested that mild forms of depression are common in this group. Certainly we know that suicide is a rapidly increasing problem among college students, and it is also possible that to some extent the dropout problem is a consequence of depression. The increasing use of drugs in this group may also be an attempt at self-treatment, similar to the way in which alcohol is used on occasion. Although there have been no systematic studies so far, clinical observation suggests that many students are depressed in response to their perception of the world. They see it committed to a course of violence, destruction, and immorality. They have lost faith in their parents and society. These perceptions are compounded by a sense of futility. Such students feel that the "system" is too strong, that they cannot in any way alter things, that they are powerless in the face of this irresistible course. Clinical impression suggests that depression is developing as a result of a perception of the failure of the world, rather than as a result of failure of the individual.

Bonine (1966) has suggested another way in which the guilt feelings of which depressives complain can be understood. Although there is in part a genuine basis for feelings of guilt—the depressive's behavior does interfere with the lives of others—there is also a significant manipulative element to it. Bonine drew an analogy with the political technique of the "big truth": the "crimes," or worthlessness, or lack of responsibility, or inabilities of the depressive are exaggerated and distorted so that the people to whom this is directed will be forced to think that adequate grounds for guilt do not exist. In this way, Bonine suggests, the depressive relieves himself of responsibility for bringing about a change in his behavior as well as the responsibility for the consequence of his destructive behavior.

Loss

Redlich and Freedman (1966) wrote, "Since Freud, it has been assumed with some conviction that depressions are reactions to losses and separations. We believe that losses and separations that occur early in life produce childhood depressions and predispose an individual to depression in adult life, which may be triggered off by a relatively minor traumatic stimulus."

A number of studies have been conducted in an attempt to determine the nature of the relationship between the development of depression in adults and the loss of a parent during childhood.

One particular problem relates to the way in which loss of the parent is defined. Some workers have confined this to the specific criteria of death of a parent or a parent leaving home. However, these are unrealistically rigid criteria; parental deprivation does take many forms and can and does occur even though both the parents are in the home with the child.

Several investigators have reported an increased incidence of early parental loss in depressed patients. However, it is clear that this finding is not specific for depression; a high incidence of early parental loss has also been reported for sociopathy, schizophrenia, drug addiction, alcoholism, broken marriages, and other conditions. It seems more likely, therefore, that early bereavement causes a predisposition to the development of some form of disturbed behavior in general instead of to depression in particular. However, it may be that the nature of the loss of the parent and the time at which it occurs is of some importance in determining the specific form of psychopathology that later occurs.

It is also necessary to remember that the loss of a parent at some crucial stage of infantile development leads to considerable disruption in the social relationships of the child, in his care, and in his opportunities for interaction. For example, if a child's father dies it may force his mother to go out to work. As a result the young child may be placed in a day-care institution or left to the dubious care of an older sibling, relative, or domestic help. Even worse, he may be institutionalized. It is conceivable that this disruption, over a period of time, gives rise to the psychological deficiency that later manifests itself in adult depression or other psychological disturbances. It is the author's belief that none of the many studies on this subject have adequately controlled for these factors.

The general theory that we are considering, then, holds that adult depression is precipitated by a current loss (real or symbolic) that recapitulates the original loss and causes the adult to regress to the emotional state he was in when the original loss occurred. At this stage of our knowledge there is no clear-cut evidence to support this theory; the problem is considered in more detail in the section on the relationship between depression and stress (see page 28).

Aggression

Many early theoreticians regarded aggression as an important component of the psychopathology of depression.[1] They suggested that the inability to consciously handle feelings of aggression or, alternatively, the

[1] For a recent review, see Kendell (1970).

fear of being overwhelmed by such feelings, with consequent denial or internalization of the feelings, was central to the development of a clinical depression. Several recent writers, while conceding that there are indeed manifestations of aggressive feelings in depressed patients, have suggested that these are secondary to the development of the illness. Among them are Cohen et al. (1954) (see page 52) and Balint (1952), who suggested that the anger and bitterness seen in many depressed patients may be a consequence of their condition rather than essential to its development. They suggest that the patients' sense of frustration and suffering leads to feelings of anger, bitterness, and the wish to lash out and destroy the unknown factors responsible for their suffering.

Bonine (1966) has offered an alternative and intriguing explanation of the relationship between aggression and depression. He suggested that the depression itself is actually "one of the *forms* of expressing hostility." He points out that the effect of the depression on those with whom the patient lives is in fact punitive and revengeful. Depressives would deny that this is their intention and protest the suggestion that they are punishing those around them, but there is much in their behavior and in the patterns of interaction set up with family members to support this suggestion.

Gershon et al. (1968) have conducted one of the very few studies on the relationship between hostility and depression. They divided hostility into two types: *hostility-in* (inner-directed) and *hostility-out* (outer-directed). In a group of six depressed women whom they studied over a period of weeks, they found that there was a correlation between hostility-in and the severity of the depression in four patients. The other two women, who were regarded as having hysterical personalities, showed a correlation between severity of the depression and both hostility-in and hostility-out.

Oral Dependency

An important feature of the psychoanalytic theories of depression is the view that the depressed person has excessive oral dependency needs; that is, the depressed person has an exaggerated dependency on external sources (usually significant individuals) for support, approval, love, reassurance, and attention. He requires these sources to bolster his own self-confidence and to maintain a reasonable emotional equilibrium. Withdrawal of these supplies, or their failure to provide an appropriate increment in the face of additional stress, may lead to the development of depression in the oral-dependent individual.

All clinicians are familiar with patients whose mood states seem to fluctuate in direct relationship to the extent to which they receive external support and approval. These patients often have a history of frequent minor episodes of depression that rapidly respond to supportive psychotherapy or to appropriate environmental manipulations. These do not change the basic personality or affect the liability to future episodes. They do, however, resolve the current depression. These patients often become very dependent on their therapists and will perceive rejection in many apparently trivial incidents. For example, they may relapse when the therapist goes on vacation. Here again, however, the universality of the phenomenon is open to question.

CHAPTER SIX

SOCIAL AND CULTURAL STUDIES

A variety of social, cultural, religious, and educational factors may exert some influence on the incidence and form of the affective disorders. It is apparent that child-rearing practices, religious training, cultural patterns of mourning, the presence of socially acceptable outlets for aggression and other drives, the extent to which a culture inculcates guilt or diffuses personal responsibility, and specific genetic traits in any group of people will influence the development and form of psychopathology. The impact of these factors has not been carefully studied; thus the remarks that follow are of necessity limited and incomplete.

DECLINING INCIDENCE OF MANIC-DEPRESSIVE ILLNESS

Although the incidence of depression in the Western world is high and perhaps increasing, there has been a consistent and significant decline in the recorded incidence of manic-depressive illness. In New York State, for example, between 1928 and 1947 the recorded incidence of hospitalized manic-depressives was reduced by approximately two-thirds and may have decreased further since. This may be a real reduction in the incidence of the disorder, but it may be that the reduction is apparent and results from (1) changing criteria for diagnosis; (2) alterations in the clinical manifestations of the disorders, leading to incorrect diagnoses; (3) modification of the course of the illness by more intensive therapeutic intervention; or (4) a retention of patients with milder forms of this disorder in the community. It is possible that some of these patients present themselves for treatment with hidden depressions (see p. 16).

It is clear that mania is seen much less frequently today than in the past (except perhaps in primitive tribal societies in Africa and elsewhere). This may be either because of a decrease in manic-depressive illness or an increase in the incidence of the purely depressive form of this condition.

Arieti (1959) has suggested that there has been a *true* decrease in the incidence of manic-depressive illness and that this is related to changes in cultural factors. Responsibility and authority were vested in a minority ruling class until the influence of the doctrines of Luther and Calvin caused an increasing number of individuals to feel responsible for their own actions. With this change, "deeply felt concepts of responsibility, duty, guilt, and punishment, which up to that time had been confined to a few religious men, acquired general acceptance and tremendous significance and came to color every manifestation of life" (1959). Arieti suggested that this change was the basis of an increased frequency of depression, and that with the contemporary decline of this Puritan ethic there has been a decrease in the incidence of manic-depressive illness.

Arieti also suggested that there are important similarities between the life pattern of the manic-depressive and that of the inner-directed personality (Reisman et al., 1950). He pointed out that the gradual replacement of the inner-directed personality by the other-directed personality in recent years has paralleled the decreased incidence of manic-depressive illness. Reisman et al. have discussed the development of these two types of personalities and their differences in some detail, pointing out that the essential feature of the inner-directed personality is that motivation is derived from internal (inner) sources, having been instilled there very early in life, and that this brings such a person to "inescapably destined goals." This inevitably leads to a certain rigidity of personality and of a society dominated by this personality type. The inner-directed personality is typified by the "old middle class"—banker, tradesman, small entrepreneur. In contrast, Reisman sees the other-directed personality as a phenomenon of contemporary American life; such a person is continuously closely influenced by his contemporaries, who provide a source of direction and motivation. The sources of motivation include friends, family, and indirect pressures such as the mass media. Thus the goals toward which "the other-directed person strives shift with that guidance: it is only the process of striving itself and the process of paying close attention to the signals from others that remain unaltered throughout life." The other-directed personality is typified by the "new middle class"—bureaucrat, salaried employee in business, and so on.

HUTTERITES

The Hutterites are a small, inbred group living in the Dakotas, Montana, and the central provinces of Canada. They are an Anabaptist group dominated by marked religious strictures, and allow little opportunity for the open expression of emotions or the individualization of personality. In many ways, this is an inner-directed society. Because they live in isolated communities with very limited intermarriage, and because there is such a carefully defined code for personal and social behavior, the Hutterites present an unusual opportunity for studying the effects of social and cultural factors on various forms of psychopathology. Eaton and Weil (1955) have conducted such an investigation. They found that manic-depressive illness was four times as frequent as schizophrenia among the Hutterites. This was a very unexpected finding; the incidence of schizophrenia far exceeds that of manic-depressive illness in the general population of the United States. Consequently, it seems that there is something operating within the Hutterite community that predisposes its members to a particularly high incidence of manic-depressive illness. In view of the similarities between their culture and that of the "typical" manic-depressive culture described by Arieti and others, this is not surprising.

One word of caution must be raised: consideration must be given to the possibility that the significant inbreeding that occurs among the Hutterites may have been responsible for the high incidence of manic-depressive illness. It is well known that this type of inbreeding within a small group of people increases the likelihood of any genetic (hereditary) factors emerging.

AFRICAN SOCIETIES

Complementing these observations is an old assumption that depression is rare in Africa,[1] and that mania is relatively common. This has been explained by reference to provision in African cultures for the open expression of mourning and guilt in acceptable social forms, to the protective benefits of the extended family, and to the presence of a collective (tribal) superego instead of an individual superego.

However, these claims are based primarily on observations of a superficial nature and may well be contradicted by more careful studies. Several recent reports suggest that depression is more frequent in Africa than had been supposed, but that it has not been recognized because of an overlay of hypochondriacal and confusional symptoms. For example, Leighton and

[1] Depression is also supposed to be rare in other "primitive" societies: Java, Haiti, the Tarahumara Indians of Mexico.

his colleagues (1963) found that many of the symptoms of depression were widespread among the Yoruba tribe of Western Nigeria, and Field (1958) found depression to be common among the Ashanti in Ghana. However, there *was* a conspicuous absence of guilt and self-reproach, and the concept of depression as understood in Western communities was not part of the culture of the Yorubas. Indeed, there is no word for depression in their language.

This observation leads to the more general question of whether the presence of guilt or self-reproach is required before a diagnosis of depression can be made. According to the classical psychoanalytic concept of depression, these elements would be a sine qua non (see p. 60). However, clinical experience strongly suggests that significant depression may be present in the absence of overt guilt, and psychotherapy with many nondepressed patients will reveal guilt. Furthermore, depression in adolescents manifests many of the classical features of depression, but with an absence of guilt.

It seems likely that the content of the depression and the way in which it manifests itself is to a considerable extent affected by environment and culture. Thus, among youth, it often manifests in such behavior as dropping out of school or drug abuse, and among Africans living in a tribal society it may manifest itself in hypochondriasis and multiple and occasionally bizarre somatic symptomatology.

Leighton et al. (1963) provide a number of striking case reports. For example, they described a 48-year-old Yoruba woman whose feelings of hopelessness and despair were sufficient for her to want to die. In addition, she had difficulties in making decisions, found herself withdrawing from the social company she had previously enjoyed, worried constantly, was tired, and had poor appetite and lost weight. A 63-year-old Yoruba tribesman, who had not spontaneously complained of difficulties, reported feelings of despair, tiredness, preoccupation with money and the criticisms he felt others had been directing at him for about three years. These feelings had become intertwined with fears of malignant supernatural powers and witchcraft.

Collomb (1967) reviewed the literature on the incidence of depression in various parts of Africa. Differences in methodology and in the theoretical orientations of the researchers resulted in reports of incidence rates varying between 1.1 and 15 percent. Collomb points out the problems that arise as a result of the failure of the investigators to allow for the vital role of the local culture on the form of the illness. He suggests that for many Africans "the depressive frame of mind is absorbed by, or invested into, systems of persecution or of somatic complaints," with a consequent absence of guilt feelings, self-accusation, devaluation, incapacity, and suicidal behavior.

AFRO-AMERICANS

It has also been suggested that depression is relatively uncommon among southern Afro-Americans. Vitols (1961) reviewed patterns of psychiatric illness and concluded that depression and suicide are rare in the southern black community compared with both southern whites and northern blacks. The U. S. Department of Statistics for 1959 reports that suicide rates (which, as suggested earlier—see p. 13—probably partially reflect the incidence of depression) vary significantly between these groups.

Table 5 shows that the *recorded* suicide rate among southern blacks is only 25 percent of that among southern whites. There is no significant difference in the suicide rates between all four white groups and northern blacks.

Vitols suggests that the reported low incidence of depression and suicide among southern blacks might arise from the fact that they have less to lose (in terms of "object loss") and are less likely to lose it. He postulates other reasons for the reported low incidence: limited expectation and aspiration on the part of the southern black; protection afforded by a fundamentalist religious practice, which provides opportunity for adequate grieving; and the support of the extended family, which is more widespread in the southern black community than in other groups. However, he offers little objective evidence to support these contentions.

The figures for black suicide and depression in the South may well be misleading. A wide difference in social, cultural, and economic factors between regional and racial groups probably causes differences in the rates of hospital admissions, and the standard statistics will not reflect the true incidence of the condition.

A recent study of the effects of racial integration on some Southern psychiatric hospitals found that there was a much higher incidence of psychotic depression among new black patients admitted to the hospitals than previous statistics had revealed (McGough et al., 1967). It is therefore

TABLE 5: Incidence of Suicide in the United States (per 100,000 of population per year)[a]

Region	White	Black
New England	10.4	9.2
South Atlantic	11.9	4.0
East South Central	9.9	2.8
West South Central	9.4	3.2

[a] U. S. Department of Statistics (1959).

possible that the low incidence reported for southern blacks is a spurious finding that will disappear with social change.

Mania is about one-third as common among blacks as among whites in the United States. This is thought to be a national phenomenon and not regionally restricted. It may be that the particular variety of affective illness known as manic-depressive illness is less common among blacks than whites. This could result from differences in the distribution of the genes that predispose to this illness in the two racial groups (see Chapter 9); it need not have any effect on the incidence of other varieties of depression among blacks. Alternatively, it may be that manic-depressive illness is as common among blacks as it is among whites but that it usually is manifested in the depressed form and only rarely as mania.

Hendin (1969) reported that the suicide rate among young Afro-American men (age 20 to 35) in New York City is twice as high as that among white men of the same age group. Hendin suggested that this finding is not surprising in view of the fact that "a sense of despair, a feeling that life will never be satisfying, confronts so many blacks at a far younger age than it does most whites." He points out that the largest number of suicides among whites in New York City occurs after the age of 45, when they have passed through a significant portion of their adult lives and have reached a state in which they anticipate decline; young blacks in New York experience a sense of despair and anticipation of decline at a relatively early age. Those who survive the first three decades of life have presumably made some accommodation, which usually involves a scaling down of aspirations; consequently, Hendin suggests, the suicide rate decreases.

OTHER SOCIOCULTURAL GROUPS

Observations have also been made on the incidence and form of affective disorders in other sociocultural groups. Generally, these claims have not been substantiated by careful study.

1. Manic-depressive illness has been reported as especially frequent among Jews. Recently some question has been raised about the universality of this claim (Grewel, 1967).

2. Several investigators (Yap, 1958; Lin, 1953) have reported that depression among the Japanese and the Chinese is usually not accompanied by as many ideas of guilt and sin as in Western societies. Yap (1965) reported that affective disorders among Hong Kong Chinese are indistinguishable from those in the West.

3. Depression is often thought to be more frequent among higher socio-economic groups. However, the possibility that this reflects the bias of clinicians is supported by a report by Schwab et al. (1967), who showed that symptoms of depression were at least as common (if not more so) in patients of a lower socio-economic class.

CHAPTER SEVEN

BIOCHEMICAL STUDIES

Cognitive and emotional activities are always accompanied by biological changes in the central or autonomic nervous systems and/or in the endocrine glands. Whether psychopathology is primarily psychological or biological in origin, whether the primary symptoms are in the realm of mood, behavior, or cognition, there is always some activity and change in biological systems.

We do not yet have techniques sufficiently sophisticated to bridge the gap between the expression of behavior on one hand and the underlying biological activity on the other. It is important to remember that even if it is demonstrated that changes in one or other biological system occur in association with a particular psychological state, the problem remains of whether the biological change is primary or whether it is a consequence. Further, the complexity of the biological systems associated with the expression of affect and behavior is such that we are still not able to determine the precise relationships among the various systems that are known to be involved.

In the last century a group of psychiatric diseases with observable neuropathology has been separated from the so-called functional illnesses. (The term *functional* is used to denote conditions for which no physical cause can be found, with the implied assumption that they are psychological in origin). General paresis of the insane (GPI) was once classed as a functional psychiatric illness. Patients with this condition presented multiple changes in behavior, mood, and intellect, and were assumed to be suffering from an unknown psychological disorder. However, the realization that GPI was in fact a neurological complication of syphilis made it necessary to drop this approach.

Depression is usually classed with the functional illnesses, reflecting the widespread belief that it is primarily psychological in origin. In recent years this practice has been subjected to questioning. Numerous studies have shown that there is a biology of depression and that drugs, which presumably act through biological systems, affect the course of depression. However, no definitive findings have emerged. It is probable that in the next few years advances in technology coupled with new hypotheses will cause a rapid expansion of research in this area. The fact that constant biological changes have not yet been demonstrated in patients with depression does not mean that subtle biochemical abnormalities, such as those involving enzyme systems, may not be present. Likewise it is important to remember that the demonstration of such changes would not in itself exclude the possibility that they were secondary to a functional disorder. For example, we know that stressful experiences will cause changes in cortisol and norepinephrine (noradrenalin) metabolism (among others). These changes can be measured. Whether the emotions felt at the time of the stress experience result from the stress *per se* or from a specific action of these hormones is uncertain. Until recently it was thought that the changes are associated with specific subjective emotional feelings, but recent work by Schachter (1964) suggests that they simply serve to prime us for the experience of an emotion. The particular emotion experienced is determined by the perception of the events at this time, rather than by the biochemical changes.

The investigation of biological systems in psychiatric patients poses numerous problems. First, we assume that the essential biological abnormality is within the central nervous system, probably in the brain. Our ability to study the human brain in its functioning state is extremely limited. For example, if we wish to know the level of a particular enzyme or hormone in the brain, we will, in most cases, measure the amount of that substance in the blood or the urine of the subject. This means that we are actually measuring the level and activity of this substance in the whole body. Consequently, a small but significant abnormality in a particular part of the brain may be obscured through averaging if the substance is functioning at normal levels in the rest of the body.

Furthermore, an infinite number of variables can affect the particular biological system being studied. It is therefore necessary to control for such factors as diet, activity levels, fear, stress, sleep, body size, stage and severity of the illness, treatment procedures, kidney and liver function, and a host of other variables; it is almost impossible to control for all these variables in any one study. As a result there have been several studies in which apparently significant findings have been reported, but the findings are later shown to result from such factors as peculiarities in hospital diet, or to patients' reactions to being hospitalized, or even to conditions of the study itself. Many of these problems of control apply equally to studies of psychological dysfunction in depression.

A number of biological changes have been noted in patients with affective disorders. Others are implied from indirect information. Some of these changes are discussed in the following sections.

ADRENOCORTICAL HORMONE METABOLISM

The adrenal glands are small endocrine glands situated above each kidney. An endocrine gland releases its hormones directly into the blood, which rapidly distributes the hormone throughout the body, allowing it to exert an effect on distant organs and tissues. The adrenal cortex produces a large number of steroid hormones (so named because of their basic molecular structure). Of these, hydrocortisone—*cortisol*—is the one with which we shall be concerned.

Several studies have demonstrated that there is an increased production of cortisol in depressed patients (Rubin and Mandell, 1967). Claims have been made that the extent of the increase correlates with the severity of the illness, but this is uncertain. Bunney et al. (1965) have studied a group of patients with recurrent psychotic depressive episodes. They found an association between the onset of each episode and an increase in cortisol production. They also studied a patient who manifested remarkably consistent 48-hour manic and depressive cycles, in whom they showed a definite relationship between cortisol levels and mood state. There was an elevation in cortisol levels during the depressed phase and a reduction during the manic phase. Similar findings have been reported by other workers. However, it should be noted that in most studies there are usually a number of patients who do not show any significant alteration in cortisol levels.

It has been suggested that the changes in cortisol production might contribute to the development of the affective disorders. This is not likely. It is known that cortisol production is increased in a number of conditions that involve stress. For example, agitated schizophrenics and patients with anxiety states are two types of psychiatric patients who may have elevated cortisol levels. Hospitalization for relatively innocuous conditions may cause an increase in cortisol production, as do such events as combat, examinations, and watching stressful movies. It seems probable that the increase in cortisol production observed in some depressed patients is a nonspecific stress response.

Sachar (1967) has reported evidence that supports this interpretation. He has shown that the elevation in cortisol production in depressed patients is significantly correlated with the subjective experience of stress and distress. By monitoring cortisol levels of depressed patients during psychotherapy, he showed that they were within normal range most of the time. However, on occasions when a patient experienced some insight into the nature of his condition and of some of the psychodynamic factors associated with it, there were marked increases in cortisol levels. Sachar suggested that the efficient operation of defense mechanisms to deny significant stressful events associated with the depression serves to keep steroid levels within normal limits and to reduce subjective distress. Breaching these defense mechanisms is associated with an elevation in cortisol production.

The metabolism of other steroid hormones in depression has not been studied as systematically as has that of cortisol. However, some observations are relevant. Depression is more frequent in women than in men; depression in both men and women frequently occurs during the involutional period when there are significant changes in various hormones; and there are reports that the oral contraceptive compounds (usually a combination of estrogen and progesterone, two steroid hormones) both cause depression and, paradoxically, relieve depressive symptoms. There is also evidence to suggest that progesterone, a sex hormone produced mainly by the ovaries and vital for normal female sexual and reproductive functioning, may be classed with the male steroid hormones or androgens. Finally, it is known that progesterones, androgen (male sex hormone), and estrogen all have a sedative effect on the central nervous system. These observations do not provide any substantial proof, but they do support the hypothesis that alterations either in the amounts of these sex hormones or of their relative proportions could produce or contribute to mood and behavioral changes (Mendels, 1969).

ELECTROLYTE METABOLISM

Electrolytes, or electrically charged atoms, played a vital role in the normal functioning of the nervous system. The main emphasis of research in this area has been on the study of sodium and potassium metabolism, and there has been some preliminary work on aspects of calcium and magnesium metabolism in depressed patients.

Sodium, Potassium, and Water Distribution

Several important electrolytes are unevenly distributed on either side of the membrane of a nerve cell (neuron). There is a higher concentration of sodium outside the nerve cell and a higher concentration of potassium ions inside the cell.

The difference is of vital importance in the maintenance of what is known as the *resting potential* of the cell. For equilibrium to exist, there must be a balance in the electrical charge of the atoms outside the cell and the atoms inside the cell. Changes in the distribution of sodium and potassium lead to changes in the resting potential of the cell, which in turn affects its excitability.[1] The normal distribution of sodium and potassium is maintained by an active metabolic process known as the *sodium pump*. It requires an appropriate stimulus along the nerves to alter this distribution and thus to initiate a nerve impulse.

Any factor that alters sodium or potassium metabolism, their concentrations on either side of the neuronal membrane, or their capacity to respond in an appropriate fashion to stimuli, will affect the functioning of the neurons, particularly their excitability. This in turn may affect any aspect of central nervous system function and of human behavior. Other electrolytes (for example, calcium) and several hormones (for instance, norepinephrine, serotonin) also have an important role in nerve impulse generation and the propagation of the impulse along the nerve fiber; some of these are discussed later.

Coppen (1965) and Shaw (1966) have demonstrated that there may be a disturbance in the distribution of sodium and potassium in depressed (and manic) patients. They reported an increase in the intracellular sodium in patients with psychotic depression. There was a corresponding decrease in the intracellular sodium after clinical recovery. Potassium did not change significantly. Similar findings, but of greater magnitude, were reported for a group of manic patients. The evidence available suggested that these changes resulted from a redistribution of the electrolytes within the body, and not to a change in the total body concentrations of sodium and potassium.

The disturbance of sodium distribution described by these workers was considerable and, if confirmed, would have major implications for our understanding of the affective disorders. For example, an increase in intracellular sodium of the degree they have reported would cause a reduction in the average resting potential of the neurons with a consequent increase in neuronal excitability; that is, a smaller stimulus than normal could cause the neurons to discharge and a nerve impulse to be propagated.

These findings have given rise to the hypothesis that there is an *unstable hyperexcitability* of the central nervous system (or parts of it) in de-

---

[1] Excitability is the strength of the stimulus required to cause a neuron to set up a nerve impulse, the wave of electrical activity that is propagated along the nerve fiber to the next neuron or to the target organ.

pression and possibly in mania (Whybrow and Mendels, 1969). This implies that it would require a *smaller* stimulus than normal to set up a nerve impulse. The work of several investigators in the neurophysiology of depression gives indirect support to this hypothesis (see Chapter 8).

Changes in sodium (and potassium) distribution could arise in several ways. It is known that sodium distribution is affected by such hormones as cortisol, progesterone, aldosterone (a hormone produced by the adrenal gland and responsible for aspects of kidney functioning, particularly those relating to electrolyte balance), and by antidiuretic hormone (which is produced by the pituitary gland and plays an important role in kidney functioning and water and electrolyte balance).

Clinical and animal studies also show that cortisol and ACTH (adrenocorticotrophic hormone produced by the pituitary gland, controlling aspects of adrenal gland hormone production, particularly cortisol) can increase brain excitability. Further, the distribution of these electrolytes has an important effect on the functioning of a group of neurohormones known as the catecholamines. There is considerable indirect evidence that the catecholamines may be disturbed in patients with affective disorders (see p. 77).

The successful treatment of mania (and possibly depression) with lithium salts is of interest. Lithium has many of the properties of sodium and can substitute for it in many ways. Coppen (1965) has shown that lithium apparently produces a marked reduction in intracellular sodium, and therefore may correct pathological changes in its distribution. There is also some evidence that lithium reduces central nervous system excitability (Whybrow and Mendels, 1969).

Calcium Metabolism

Flach has shown that the response to treatment (electroconvulsive therapy or the antidepressant drug imipramine, see Chapter 11) in a group of 57 patients with affective disorders, paranoid schizophrenic reaction, and psychoneurotic reaction was associated with significant changes in the amount of calcium excreted in the urine. There was a significant reduction in the amount of calcium excreted in the urine of patients who improved, as compared with a small rise in urinary calcium excretion in patients who did not respond to treatment; that is, clinical improvement was associated with calcium retention. This change was independent of sex or mode of treatment. In further studies using intravenous radioactive calcium (Ca^{47}) in a group of six patients with a diagnosis of endogenous depression, he confirmed the association between a tendency to retain calcium in the body (to excrete less of it in the urine) and clinical improvement (Flach, 1968).

These findings are of considerable interest, but must await confirmation from other investigators.

Calcium plays an important role in the normal functioning of nerve cells. Among other things, it serves to regulate sodium and potassium passage across the cell membrane. If the reported increase in calcium retention associated with recovery in depressed patients were paralleled by an increase in calcium concentration at the cell membrane, sodium and potassium passage across that membrane would be influenced. It is possible, then, that during depression there is a relative deficiency of calcium at the cell membrane (as more is being lost through the urine), allowing sodium to pass into the cell in increased amounts and leading to the raised intracellular sodium discussed above. With recovery there would be a decrease in calcium excretion, an increased calcium retention in the body, and a possible increase in the amount of sodium able to pass into the cell. This would then lead to a decrease in intracellular sodium from the previous abnormal high and a return to normal levels.

BIOGENIC AMINE METABOLISM

Considerable attention is being directed toward the relationship between mood and biogenic amine activity. The biogenic amines are a group of hormones that play several vital roles in central nervous system functioning. Historically our attention was first directed to the importance of these amines in the study of human behavior, when Walter Cannon in 1915 postulated that epinephrine (adrenalin) was secreted as part of an animal's response to rage and fear-inducing situations. Since then the intimate involvement of this and other amines in many aspects of central and peripheral nervous function has become apparent.

The amines can be divided into two broad groups according to their basic chemical structure:

1. *Catecholamines,* such as epinephrine, norepinephrine, and dopamine; and

2. *Indole amines,* such as serotonin (5 hydroxy-tryptamine) and histamine.

The amines have been implicated as having a possible role in the genesis of depression for several reasons.

1. Drugs used in the treatment of depression increase the level of available amines in the brain.

2. Drugs known to increase the level of brain amines produce overactivity and alertness in experimental animals.

3. Drugs (such as reserpine) known to deplete the brain amines produce sedation and inactivity in experimental animals.

4. Drugs that deplete brain amines cause depression in man.

Thus, although no direct cause and effect relationship has been shown, there is an increasing body of indirect evidence of a relationship between depression and the level of functioning biogenic amines in the brain.

The amines play an important role in the formation of impulses at neurons as well as impulse transmission along the nerve fiber. In general, increased neuronal activity will increase the rate of amine turnover (perhaps particularly norepinephrine metabolism). If this increased rate of production continues for any length of time, the possibility exists that, at least in some individuals, there is a rate-limiting step in its synthesis. In other words, one stage in the manufacture or use of an amine in the body proceeds at a slower rate than all the other stages in its metabolism. This would serve as a bottleneck, and the rate of production and utilization of the particular hormone would be determined by it. Should the demand for hormone increase beyond the capacity of this rate-limiting step, there would be a functional insufficiency. Although the absolute concentration of the hormone would be above the normal level, it would not be sufficient in view of the increased need; this would result in a relative impairment of functioning. Further, if there were a chronic increase in demand and turnover, there might be an exhaustion of the metabolic process, with a consequent real decrease in production and reduced level of amine.

At this time researchers have concentrated their attention on one particular amine—the catecholamine, norepinephrine. Schildkraut (1965) has proposed the catecholamine hypothesis of affective disorders, in which he states that, "some, if not all, depressions are associated with an absolute or relative deficiency of catecholamines, particularly norepinephrine, at functionally important receptor sites in the brain. Elation conversely may be associated with an excess of such amines."

The catecholamine hypothesis is of necessity largely based on the indirect pharmacological evidence outlined above, as it is obviously impossible to study the levels of particular catecholamines in significant areas of the brain of depressed patients.

Although the bulk of research work in this area has been directed toward norepinephrine, much of the evidence used to implicate this amine as an important agent in the genesis of mood change could, with almost equal validity, be applied to other amines; the drugs that relieve depression and those that induce it affect amines other than norepinephrine, for example, serotonin (Glassman, 1969).

There is some additional evidence to support the possibility that there is a disturbance of serotonin metabolism in some depressed patients. In addition to the fact that the mood-altering drugs cause changes in serotonin metabolism, it has been shown that:

1. Tryptophan relieves depression in some people. Tryptophan is converted by the body into serotonin. The fact that it relieves depression therefore increases the likelihood that there is an abnormality of serotonin metabolism in depression.

2. There is a decreased amount of the normal breakdown products (excretory products formed as the serotonin is being used) of serotonin in depressives. Among the several ways in which this could arise are a reduced amount of serotonin in the body or a decrease in its utilization.

It is important to realize that even if it is clearly demonstrated that one or more of the biogenic amines is functioning abnormally in people with depression, this will not constitute proof that the disturbance is the cause of the condition. For example, several recent reports suggest that changes in amine metabolism may be part of a nonspecific response to stress instead of to depression. Bliss et al. (1966) found that animals subjected to a wide variety of stresses have a reduction in the concentration of brain norepinephrine. This decrease occurred irrespective of the nature of the animal's mood response to the experimental procedure: both pleasurable and dysphoric states were associated with comparable reductions in brain norepinephrine. Bliss et al. therefore suggested that "emotionality in animals appears to reduce the concentration of norepinephrine in the brain."

OTHER BIOCHEMICAL CHANGES

A number of other biochemical changes have been reported in depressed patients. So far these are relatively isolated observations. At least some of them may be secondary consequences of changes such as the increase in adrenocortical hormone production that occurs in depressed patients. Among the reports are:

1. *Alterations in the way in which glucose is utilized by the body* (Van Praag & Leisnse, 1965). As glucose is the basic source of all energy in the body, this may be important.

2. *A significant increase in the amount of acetaldehyde in the blood*

(Assael, 1964). This could in part reflect changes in carbohydrate (especially glucose) metabolism and may therefore be related to item 1.

3. *A significant correlation between the level of blood acetyl-methyl carbinol and the severity of depression* (McC. Anderson & Dawson, 1962). Acetyl-methyl carbinol is an end product of glucose metabolism in the body.

4. *A significant increase in plasma magnesium levels in depressed patients* (not in manic patients), which persisted after clinical remission (Cade, 1964).

5. *A significant increase in plasma triglycerides* (fatty acids) in manic-depressive men as compared with control subjects, and *an increase in plasma cholesterol* in both manic-depressive males and females. These changes were not statistically significant for the female subjects (Brandrup and Randrup, 1967).

IN SUMMARY

Evidence suggests that depressed patients have potentially important changes in the metabolism of one or more of the biogenic amines (especially norepinephrine and serotonin), in certain electrolytes (especially sodium and potassium), and in one or more steroid hormones. It is probable that other biochemical changes take place as well. We know that although these are apparently distinct systems in the body's biochemistry, they are all closely functionally interrelated. Thus we cannot at this time say which of these changes are primary and which secondary. Indeed, all of the changes described in this chapter may be the result of an unrecognized biochemical change or the result of psychological and stress factors.

CHAPTER EIGHT

PSYCHOPHYSIOLOGY

Psychophysiology is the study of the relationship between behavior and physiology. Usually it is concerned with measuring changes in a particular physiological function that occur with changes in behavior, mood, or function. The following are among the psychophysiological studies conducted with depressives.

ELECTROENCEPHALOGRAPHIC STUDIES (EEG)

The electroencephalograph is used to record the electrical activity of the brain. Every time a neuron (nerve cell) in the brain is activated it generates a tiny electrical charge. The accumulated activity from millions of brain cells generates an electrical current that is powerful enough to be recorded by electrodes placed on the skull. The resultant EEG record reflects the varying degrees of activity in different areas of the brain over time.

Electroencephalographic studies of depressed patients have been conducted while the subjects were awake and resting quietly, asleep, and under other specialized conditions (such as arousal responses and evoked potentials). Some of the findings from these studies and their implications are discussed below.

Resting EEG

When a subject sits quietly in a comfortable chair with his eyes closed and with no significant external stimuli impinging on him, the EEG will show a fairly regular rhythm of 8 to 13 cycles per second (cps). This is the *resting alpha rhythm.*

No consistent abnormalities have been found in the resting EEG of depressed or manic patients. Although several investigators claim to have demonstrated EEG abnormalities, their claims must be regarded with caution; the studies usually involved poorly defined patient groups and inadequately controlled conditions. Denber (1958) surveyed the EEGs obtained from a large number of psychiatric patients and, although he questioned the existence of specific electroencephalographic patterns for particular psychiatric groups, he suggested that there was evidence for a basic but nonspecific "electrophysiologic instability" existing in the depressed patient. It is possible that, with the future development of more sophisticated methods of recording EEGs and of computerized methods of scoring the records, more significant findings may emerge.

Arousal Response

The term *arousal response* refers to interruption of the EEG resting pattern by an auditory, visual, or other stimulus. That is, the alpha rhythm can easily be blocked if a resting subject begins to concentrate on a problem, hears a noise, or opens his eyes and looks around. This will produce changes in the EEG pattern. The nature of the arousal response is affected by a variety of factors, including the state of excitability of the central nervous system and the emotional and cognitive set of the subject.

Eleven patients were studied while depressed and after treatment by Paulson and Gottlieb (1961), who found that (1) the mean latency of the arousal response (the time from stimulation to suppression of the alpha rhythm) was the same during depression and after clinical recovery; (2) blocking (alpha suppression) lasted significantly longer during depression than after recovery; and (3) there was a reduction in the number of arousal responses during the depressive phase. Other investigators have also reported a significant prolongation of the alpha suppression in depressed patients.

Evoked Potential

If the back of a person's hand is touched by a feather, the local nerve endings are stimulated, and a message is sent along the nerves in the hand, up the arm and through to that part of the brain, in the cerebral cortex or grey matter, responsible for recognizing and recording peripheral sensations. This is accompanied by local electrical activity in the cortex. This slight impulse cannot be recorded by a conventional EEG. However, if the stimulus to the hand is repeated a number of times in a regular fashion it is possible to detect the repeated messages that arrive at the cerebral cortex by a process of averaging; the repetitive stimuli are identical and will stand out from the multiple other irregular activities in this part of the brain. This measurement is known as an *evoked potential or sensory evoked response.*

The procedure can be extended by the application of two separate stimuli to the same part of the hand in order to determine the length of the *refractory period,* which is the recovery time required after the first stimulus before a complete response can be obtained to the second.

Shagass and Schwartz (1962) found that the initial recovery of cerebral cortical activity in normal subjects occurred within 20 milliseconds (msec) of the initial stimulus, followed by a period of diminished responsiveness to further stimuli with a second peak of recovery at about 120 msec. Fifteen depressed patients with a mean age of 55 years, diagnosed as having a psychotic depressive illness (either manic-depressive or involutional psychosis), failed to recover full responsiveness during the first 20 msec; that is, it took longer before there could be a complete response to the next stimulus. Compared with the controls, the depressives showed a mean recovery of cortical reactivity of less than 50 percent at any time before 20 msec. When retested after successful treatment, they showed a shift toward a normal cortical reactivity pattern. Studies of patients with other psychiatric disorders also showed significant deviations from normal cortical reactivity. However, it was only in patients diagnosed as psychotic depressives that a consistent deficiency in recovery of full responsiveness during the first 20 msec was found.

Comment on EEG Studies

Most of the claims described in the last sections must be interpreted with caution. Frequently there was inadequate definition of the patient group studied and absence of control for such important variables as age. However, some agreement on the implications can be drawn from these studies. The findings can be accounted for by a hypothesis that some depressed patients are in a state of unstable neurophysiological hyperexcitability.

This hypothesis suggests that depression is associated with a reduced threshold for neuronal discharge (a smaller stimulus is required to cause a neuron or nerve cell to discharge), and the refractory or recovery period after such a discharge is longer than normal (Whybrow and Mendels, 1969).

On this basis, the prolongation of the recovery phase beyond 20 msec found by Shagass and Schwartz in depressed patients may represent a prolongation of the refractory period. Their findings, similar to those described for the studies of arousal responses, suggest the possibility of an increased activity of the reticular activating system (the arousal portion) of the brain. The prolonged blocking of the alpha rhythm (arousal response) could be similarly explained.

PSYCHOPHYSIOLOGY OF SLEEP

Sleep disturbance is a significant feature in most descriptions of depression. Indeed, some people attribute diagnostic or therapeutic implications to the nature of the sleep disturbance. For example, it has been claimed that early morning wakening is associated with endogenous depression, whereas difficult in falling asleep is associated with reactive depression; that sleeplessness indicates that electroconvulsive therapy may be useful as a treatment; and so on. Most of these claims are based on nurses' reports of patients' sleep habits in hospitals and from patients' reports of their own sleep habits. Such methods for studying sleep patterns are highly unreliable.

The development of the electroencephalogram made possible a more precise and detailed study of sleep patterns. In an EEG study of sleep, subjects are monitored for several consecutive nights under controlled environmental conditions. The data obtained from measuring the electroencephalogram, muscle tension (EMG) (see p. 87), and eye movements can be used to recognize stages in the night's sleep. The Dement-Kleitman (1957) system is widely used for this purpose. According to this system, the night's sleep is divided into five stages that are differentiated from each other by the speed (frequency) and the size (amplitude) of the EEG waves, EMG activity, and eye movements. Stage 1 sleep consists of low-amplitude, high-frequency EEG. It is light sleep and occupies a small portion of the night. Stage 2 sleep occupies the major portion of the night and is characterized by the presence of *sleep spindles,* short bursts of fast EEG activity (14 to 16 cps). Stages 3 and 4 sleep (also referred to as *slow-wave sleep*) are periods in which the EEG is dominated by slow (1–4 cps), high-amplitude delta waves. Slow-wave sleep is generally regarded as deep sleep. The other major stage of sleep is rapid eye movement sleep (Stage 1 REM), which is characterized by the presence of periodic bursts of horizontal, jerky eye movements, fast EEG activity, and the absence of muscle potential. Dreaming occurs mainly during this stage of sleep, which occupies about 20 percent of the average night's sleep.

It is generally accepted that Stage 1 REM sleep and slow-wave sleep are two physiologically distinct states, each with its own central nervous system mechanism of control and with its individual functions. Experimental sleep-deprivation studies have shown that normal individuals require both slow-wave sleep and Stage 1 REM sleep; deprivation of either of

TABLE 6: Time in Sleep Stages

	Control Subjects		Depressed Patients		P	
	Mean Time (Minutes)	%	Mean Time (Minutes)	%	Time	%
Total sleep period	431		398.3		ns	
Actual sleep period	414.9		327.6		0.01	
Awake	6.0	1.3	40.8	10.9	0.01	0.01
Drowsy	10.6	2.4	29.9	7.1	0.05	0.01
Stage 1	4.4	1.0	11.8	3.0	ns	ns
Stage 2	160.3	36.6	160.5	40.2	ns	ns
Stage 3	62.3	14.4	58.9	15.0	ns	ns
Stage 4	80.8	19.7	20.0	4.7	0.01	0.01
Stage 1 REM	106.6	24.6	76.4	19.1	0.01	0.05

ns = not significant

these leads to the development of a marked pressure to achieve that stage of sleep. When a subject is allowed to reach the stage of which he has been deprived for a period, there is a period of compensation in which he spends extra time in that stage of sleep as if to make up for the lost time.

Mendels and Hawkins (1969) have reported on the sleep pattern of depressed patients studied shortly after admission to hospital, compared with the sleep patterns of control subjects. Table 6 shows the mean time spent in the Total Sleep Period (time from the first minute of Drowsy to the last minute of sleep); the Actual Sleep Period (Total Sleep Period minus time Awake and Drowsy); and the time spent in Stages Awake, Drowsy, 1, 2, 3, 4, and 1 REM sleep. It also shows the time spent in each stage of sleep, expressed as a percentage of the Total Sleep Period. The last columns (P) show whether the difference between the controls and the depressed patients was statistically significant. Depressed patients spent significantly less time in the Total Sleep Period, the Actual Sleep Period, Stage 1 REM, and Stage 4 sleep. They spent significantly more time Awake and Drowsy. It can be seen that some of the differences between the two groups are pronounced.

It has also been shown that depressives take longer to fall asleep, wake more frequently during the night, and wake earlier in the morning.

The sleep of 13 of the depressives was again studied after significant clinical improvement had occurred, just before their discharge from the hospital, a mean of 47.1 days after the initial study. Although their sleep had improved considerably, they continued to have significantly less slow-wave sleep (Stages 3 and 4), more time Awake and Drowsy, and more spontaneous awakenings; that is, they continued to sleep less deeply than control subjects. Of particular interest was the continued deficiency in slow-wave sleep. While the control subjects slept a mean of 80.8 minutes a night in Stage 4, the depressives slept 20.0 minutes per night during the initial study, and at follow-up time slept only 37.8 minutes per night. It can be seen that even after significant clinical improvement had occurred, the depressed patients had only half the normal amount of Stage 4 sleep. Several patients studied more intensively and followed up for a longer period continued to show a persistent deficiency of slow-wave sleep.

There is general agreement between the Mendels and Hawkins study and reports by other investigators on several important findings: there was an increased sleep latency (time taken to fall asleep) and more wakefulness in depressives than in the control subjects. The amount of Stage 1 REM sleep varied considerably. Some nights there was virtually none, whereas on other nights the patients had more than twice the normal amount. It has been suggested that this disturbance may be important in the development of depression. Slow-wave sleep was the most consistently reduced parameter in depressed patients, and the slowest to return to normal.

This difficulty in achieving slow-wave sleep, together with such manifestations of sleep disturbance as more time Awake and Drowsy, more spontaneous awakenings, more time awake in the early hours of the morning (after several hours of sleep have reduced the intensity of need), suggests that some depressives have a disturbance of the central mechanisms involved in achieving slow wave sleep. This might be because of either heightened activity of central arousal mechanisms or impaired functioning of sleep centers.

Thus far only one manic patient not receiving drug therapy has been studied in the sleep laboratory. This was a 45-year-old man who had had several previous hospitalizations for mania. He was studied for 17 nights out of a 25-night period during which the intensity of the mania increased. In most regards his sleep pattern was the same as that for the most severely depressed patients studied. There was a marked reduction in slow-wave sleep and a moderate reduction in Stage 1 REM. One of the most striking features was the extremely low arousal threshold; that is, he was very easily awakened.

The marked disturbances in the sleep of depressives, and the possibility that some of these disturbances persist even after the patients have improved clinically, has given rise to speculation as to whether these disturbances in some way contribute to the development or to the perpetuation of the depression.

ELECTROMYOGRAPHIC STUDIES (EMG)

Muscle tension or *residual motor activity* can be measured with an elec-tromygraph, which measures the electrical activity in a muscle at rest. Whatmore and Ellis (1959, 1962) reported a series of studies in which they measured muscle tension in groups of depressed and schizophrenic patients at various stages of the illness and after recovery. Although resid-ual motor activity was abnormally high in both groups of patients, a con-sistent and sustained increase in muscle tension was observed only in the depressed patients. This increase was found in both agitated and retarded depressives, but it was most marked in the extremely retarded patients.

When depressed patients received electroconvulsive therapy, a temporary decrease in muscle tension paralleled clinical improvement. However, muscle tension did not return to normal levels in the most retarded pa-tients studied, even after their recovery. Whatmore and Ellis also noted that there was a rise in muscle tension before a relapse of the depression.

Whatmore has used the term *hyperponesis* to describe the hyperactivity in the part of the nervous system that is responsible for this increase in muscle tension. This is in keeping with the hypothesis that there is a state of central nervous system hyperexcitability in some depressives.

Goldstein (1965) found a significantly raised muscle tension in 21 de-pressed outpatients who were compared with a control group. The patients also showed a greater electromyographic response to noise than either the control group or nondepressed psychiatric patients, despite the fact that the depressives were, behaviorally, the most inactive group.

Conflicting with these studies is a report by Rimon et al. (1966), who noted that muscle tension was inversely correlated with depressive sever-ity. This difference may have resulted from variations in the method used to measure muscle tension or differences in the group of patients studied. It is therefore necessary to await further and perhaps more adequately controlled trials before coming to any conclusions about the level of rest-ing muscle activity in depressed patients.

AUTONOMIC NERVOUS SYSTEM FUNCTIONING IN DEPRESSION

A number of researchers have suggested that there is a major disturbance of autonomic nervous system functioning in depressed patients. Campbell (1953), suggested that the vast majority of symptoms shown by manic-de-pressive patients were associated with such malfunctions. Among the symptoms he claims fall into this category are: hot flushes and/or burning of the skin; rapid heart beat; breathing difficulties; general feelings of weakness; pains and odd sensations in the neck, hands, and feet; headaches and sensations of pressure in the head; feelings of distress in the pit of the stomach; indigestion; loss of appetite; menstrual disturbances; constipation or diarrhea; decreased sexual desire and functioning. However, any of these symptoms may arise for reasons other than autonomic malfunction, and even if they are associated with autonomic malfunction, it is possible that their presence is a consequence instead of a primary disturbance.

Several workers have attempted to develop experimental techniques to detect the presence of autonomic nervous system dysfunction in depression. Others have tried to correlate the type or degree of autonomic nervous system dysfunction with a particular category of depression. Among these studies are those discussed below.

Funkenstein Test (Mecholyl Test)

The Funkenstein Test is based on the blood-pressure response to an intravenous injection of epinephrine or an intramuscular injection of methacholine (Mecholyl). Funkenstein (1962) claimed that depressed patients could be categorized according to the degree to which blood pressure increased (after epinephrine injection) or decreased (after methacholine injection), and according to the duration of this change. He further suggested that those depressed patients who manifested a prolonged reduction in blood pressure after methacholine injection constituted a specific group, and were likely to improve if treated with electroconvulsive therapy. Funkenstein indicated that the significant drop in blood pressure after the administration of methacholine resulted from an excessive secretion of epinephrine-like substances by the autonomic nervous system. Subsequent investigators have not been able to confirm these claims. Thorpe (1962) reports that the reliability of the test is poor and that many of the findings were related to age and severity of the illness instead of to a particular pathophysiology or to a positive indication of a response to ECT.

Salivation Studies

Several investigators (Busfield et al. 1961; Palmer et al., 1967) have studied the rate of saliva secretion in depressed patients. The results of these studies are inconclusive but indicate that there may be a significant reduction in salivation in depressed patients. It has been suggested that this reduction is particularly marked in patients diagnosed as manic-depressives or in patients who are severely depressed or agitated. Because of the contradictions in the published reports and the failure of some of the investigators to control for such variables as age, diet, smoking patterns, and other factors that would affect salivation rates, no conclusions can be reached.

Hypothalamic Function

The hypothalamus is a vital integrating and regulating center in the brain. It has been suggested that depression may arise as a result of a disturbance of hypothalamic functioning (Kraines, 1966). Kraines' evidence in favor of this includes the following.

1. Studies with animals and man indicate that nuclei in the hypothalamus are involved in the regulation of mood. In addition, hypothalamic lesions may result in mood disturbance, and electrical stimulation of certain hypothalamic centers (or closely adjacent areas) produces a pleasurable response, whereas stimulation of other centers only a few millimeters away produces an unpleasant response. The affective state induced by this stimulation may be very intense.

2. The hypothalamus is involved in the regulation of a number of functions that are disturbed in many depressed patients. These include appetite, sexual activity, menstruation, and so on.

3. The hypothalamus is an integral and vital part of the link between the cerebral cortex and endocrine glands such as the pituitary, adrenal, and thyroid, the functioning of which may be disturbed in depression.

Kraines (1966) reviewed much of the work in this area and has advanced the hypothesis that depression results from a persistent, gradually intensifying inhibition of the hypothalamic function. Much of the evidence he presents to support this hypothesis is based on preliminary, unconfirmed findings or is indirect in nature. Although there is little doubt that aspects of hypothalamic function are disturbed in depressed patients, there is insufficient evidence to support the contention that this disturbance is the cause of the problem. Further investigation is indicated.

CHAPTER NINE ‖

GENETICS

A number of investigators have suggested that there is a significant hereditary basis for the development of the affective disorders. In this chapter
we discuss some of the studies that have been conducted on the role of he-
redity.

TWIN STUDIES

Several studies have been concerned with the occurrence of depression
among twins and the likelihood that if one twin becomes depressed the
other will also develop a depression. The tendency for both twins to develop a depression if one does so is referred to as the *concordance rate*.
Identical twins have the same genetic endowment; therefore both will develop any disease that is controlled by a simple dominant genetic mechanism.

In a careful study of 38 twins among whom one of each pair had been
diagnosed as suffering from an endogenous affective disorder, Slater
(1953) found that there was a 57 percent concordance rate for identical
twins and a 29 percent concordance rate for nonidentical twins, allowing
for age correction[1]. Da Fonseca (1959) studied 60 pairs of twins from the
Maudsley Hospital twin register in London. Using the criterion of the

---

[1] Age correction is a statistical procedure designed to help calculate how many
people in a given population will have developed the illness when they have all passed through the age period of risk.

emergence of overt affective illness, Da Fonseca found a 60 percent concordance for identical twins and a 21 percent concordance for nonidentical twins. Extending his criteria to include mild forms of this condition, such as depressive or hypomanic personality, he found concordance rates of 75 percent for the identical twins and 38 percent for the nonidentical twins. These concordance rates for nonidentical twins are similar to those reported by Kallman (1952), both for nonidentical twins and for nontwin siblings. The similarities between nonidentical twins and nontwin siblings is to be expected; the similarity in the genetic endowment of nonidentical twins is the same as that for nontwin siblings.

Both identical twins and nonidentical twins were raised by the same sets of parents under similar conditions. The finding of a concordance rate higher (but not a 100 percent rate) in identical twins than in nonidentical twins therefore strongly suggests that genetic factors do play an important role in the transmission of depression (at least some forms of this condition); any difference in outcome between the identical and nonidentical twin groups is probably from genetic factors.

In an effort to distinguish between the contributions of genetics and family upbringing to personality and psychopathology, Shields (1962) compared the psychological state of 44 identical twins, who were separated early in life and raised separately, with 44 nonseparated identical twins. Among the separated twins there was one set that was concordant for affective disorder, and three sets discordant for affective disorder (neurotic depressive episodes). Although he obtained no statistically significant findings, Shields noted a number of interesting trends. For example, he found that the degree of concordance in the separated group was the same as in the nonseparated group for such variables as anxiety traits, emotional lability, rigidity, and cyclothymic features, strongly suggesting that the emergence of these factors was more influenced by genetic factors than by environmental factors.

INCIDENCE OF AFFECTIVE DISORDERS IN CHILDREN OF TWO PSYCHOTIC PARENTS

Elsasser (1952) reviewed the European literature reporting on the incidence of psychiatric illness in the offspring of two psychotic parents. He found 20 recorded cases in which both parents had been diagnosed as suffering from manic-depressive illness. Of 47 children over the age of 16 years born to these parents, 33 were regarded as normal. Fourteen had developed a psychotic illness, with 10 diagnosed as manic-depressive. The age-corrected risk for the emergence of manic-depressive illness in these children would therefore be about 32 percent, indicating a significant hereditary factor.

There were also 19 pairs of parents of whom one had been diagnosed as a schizophrenic and the other as a manic-depressive. Of 69 children over the age of 16 years born to these parents, 49 were regarded as normal. Nineteen were psychotic, with 8 having been diagnosed as schizophrenic, 8 as manic depressive, and three as "psychotic illness."

Several factors must be considered in the interpretation of these findings. First, the diagnoses both for parents and children should be viewed with reservation. Elsasser based his report on the diagnoses recorded by many different people; the multiple criteria that these psychiatrists presumably used in arriving at their diagnoses are certain to have varied considerably.

It is clear that there is not 100 percent incidence of manic-depressive illness in the offspring of parents who have both been diagnosed as manic-depressives. It is also of interest to note that a significant number of the offspring of two psychotic parents were regarded as normal. Although we cannot be certain that these children had no psychiatric problems, it is probable that at least some of them did not have any significant problems. This suggests that whatever the genetic mechanism may be, it does not have 100 percent penetrance; that is, it does not operate invariably. It further indicates that the presumably pathological environment and upbringing provided to these children was not in itself sufficient to produce this illness in them.

FAMILY STUDIES

Stenstedt (1952) conducted a careful family study using 288 cases with the diagnosis of manic-depressive illness (216 had received a definite diagnosis and 72 a probable diagnosis.) These figures included people who had not developed a full-blown illness but who had characteristics of the illness in a sufficient amount to justify inclusion, according to Stenstedt. The patients were drawn from a rural area in Sweden, where he estimated that the overall morbidity risk (risk of developing the illness) for manic-depressive illness was about 1 percent. He found an incidence of about 15 percent of manic-depressive illness in the parents, siblings, and children of his index cases (age-corrected figures). When he divided his subjects according to childhood experiences and environmental conditions, he found that there was a significantly increased likelihood of the illness developing if there was a history of an unfavorable childhood environment. For example, he found that when the patients and siblings had had unfavorable

GENERAL PSYCHOLOGICAL TESTS

Self-Rating

MMPI. The Minnesota Multiphasic Personality Inventory (Dahlstrom and Welsh, 1962) is the most widely used test in the self-rating category. It consists of 568 items that are scored as true or false. From this a number of scales designed to measure the degree of psychopathology present and to differentiate broad categories of psychopathology, are derived; for example, depression, hypochondriasis, conversion hysteria, masculinity-femininity, and several validity scales.

The *D* scale (Scale 2) on the MMPI measures the depth of clinical depression. This is defined as "pessimism of outlook on life and the future, feelings of hopelessness or worthlessness, slowing of thought and action, and frequently preoccupation with death and suicide."

"The original *D* Scale has proven to be a remarkably sensitive and dependable measure of clinical depression. Clinical experience has indicated that high scores are rarely inadvertent; they should be considered strongly indicative of significant levels of depression even when the person examined is overtly smiling and apparently comfortable" (Dahlstrom and Welsh, 1962). In spite of this broad approval, Dahlstrom and Welsh point out that the presence of a high score on the *D* Scale does not necessarily indicate a primary diagnosis of depression, in that patients with other conditions (such as schizophrenia) may also be depressed and have a high *D* score.

Depressed patients often have high scores on Scale 7 (psychasthenia or obsessive-compulsive features). Their scores tend to be lowest on Scale 9 (hypomania).

The MMPI *D* scale contains a number of heterogenous factors. Harris and Lingoes (1955) list five subscales: subjective depression, psychomotor retardation, complaints about physical malfunctioning, mental dullness, and brooding. O'Connor et al. (1967) identified five scales, which they labeled hypochondriasis, cycloid tendency, hostility, inferiority, and depression.

A number of workers have attempted to develop new subscales of the MMPI that would provide greater reliability for the recognition of depressed patients in general or aid in the delineation of specific subgroups of depressives. Although these subscales are not widely used, they are often more useful for specialized purposes than the *D* Scale. Among them are scales to delineate "pure" depressions, "subjective" depressions, psychomotor retardation, depressive reaction, and so on.

In an attempt to contribute to further understanding of the relationship between neurotic and psychotic depression, Rosen (1952) developed the MMPI *Dr* scale. This is derived essentially from a group of patients with a diagnosis of neurotic depressive reaction as compared with the patients with a diagnosis of psychotic depression used for the derivation of the original *D* Scale. The *Dr* Scale consists of 42 items, only four of which appear in the original *D* Scale. The *Dr* Scale employs many items relating to denial, and there is an absence of items relating to somatic concerns.

Projective Tests

Rorschach Test. This is commonly known as the "inkblot test" in which a subject is asked to describe all the shapes and objects he can discern in an abstract form. In discussing the role of the Rorschach, Rapaport et al. (1968) pointed out the following:

> The characteristic patterns of a single nosological group cannot be used as diagnostic indicators; they may or may not be necessary parts of the diagnostic picture of the group in question, but are generally far from sufficiently describing it and differentiating it from other nosological groups. Nor do the studies which lump together all kinds of "neuroses" or "depression" or "schizophrenia"—useful as they may be as first approximations—attempt to cope with the problem of validation of the test (p. 269).

Among the Rorschach responses that they suggested are associated with depression are the following.

1. A low *R* response (*R* = the total number of responses) occurs for both psychotic and neurotic depression. For example, whereas nondepressed neurotic patients average between 22 and 28 responses per card, depressed patients average between 11 and 18 responses. A low *R* is also noted in simple schizophrenics and in deteriorated paranoid schizophrenics. Holt (1968) pointed out that a low *R* is also found in many patients with addiction or character disorder problems (p. 300).

2. Failures (the failure to give any response to a card) are most common among depressed patients. A similar inhibition is found in some schizophrenic and neurasthenic patients.

3. Reaction time (the amount of time taken to respond after presentation of the card) is directly correlated with depressive psychomotor retardation and also with the inhibition present in some schizophrenics.

4. A tendency to select small areas of the card, rather than to make whole responses, is present in depressed patients. The whole responses that depressed patients make are frequently of the *Wb* type (that is, "based on a vague, general impression with a corresponding vagueness of content—X-ray films, islands, microscopic slides, etc.")

5. The *F* percent (the percentage of all the responses given that are pure form responses) is very high in depressed patients.

6. The $F+$ percent (the percentage of "good forms" of all the F responses) is relatively low among psychotic depressives. It increases in the severe neurotic depressives and increases still further in mild neurotic depressives, reaching its peak in this last group. Conversely, the $F-$ percentage is high among psychotic depressives and very low among neurotic depressives.

7. Color responses are relatively uncommon among depressed patients.

8. The M response (movement responses in which the human form is seen in motion) are very low among depressed patients. It is rare for depressed patients to produce more than one M response on a card.

9. The content of a depressed patient's responses to the Rorschach card differs from that of other psychopathological groups in the following ways: (a) there is a relatively small number of responses; (b) there is a significant percentage of P responses ("popular" responses; that is, those that "represent compliance with the thinking of the community"). It should be noted that, although the depressives will have a higher percentage of P responses than acute schizophrenics, they will have a lower mean number of actual P responses because of a generally lower number of responses; (c) there is a high incidence of stereotype in depressed patients; (d) there is a low incidence of original responses in depressed patients (also in simple schizophrenics); (e) there is a very low incidence of combination responses (that is, the linking together by association of responses to several different parts of the card) in depressives, and also in simple schizophrenics; (f) there is a low incidence of abnormal exaggerated verbalization in depressives (which is especially useful in differentiating psychotic depressives from paranoid schizophrenics); and (g) there is a high incidence in depressives of self-depreciation responses, which persist for the duration of the test unlike the transient self-depreciation that may occur in some normal or neurotic subjects.

The Thematic Apperception Test (TAT). The subject is shown a drawing depicting some human scene and asked to tell a story describing what is happening in the picture, how it developed, and what the outcome might be. This provides some understanding of the subject's own thinking. The stories developed by depressed patients are usually characterized by a considerable restriction of thoughts and ideas, with vague, brief accounts and reluctant responses to inquiries from the examiner. Specific inquiries give rise to silences or monosyllabic responses. Patients frequently interpret the pictures as unhappy, and tell stories involving depression, sin, morality, illness, and weakness. The stories may be marked by a great deal of perseveration and repetition. Rapaport et al. (1968) suggested that depressives will on occasion tell stories that represent their own wishful fantasies and that are dominated by themes of happiness, success, and love.

Word Association Test. Rapaport et al. (1968) emphasized that any particular type of associative disturbance that emerges in the course of this test cannot be given much weight as a diagnostic indicator. However, they have described features that they felt were most characteristic of depressed patients. In addition to a general slowness of reaction, the patients show a variety of close reactions,[1] particularly definitions (that is, "a multiword definition of the stimulus words"). Although the reaction times vary, depressives show very few of the quick reactions that are common among schizophrenic patients. Rapaport et al. suggest that psychotic depressives can be distinguished from neurotic depressives by an increased incidence of both close and distant reactions and by accumulation of more blocking responses. Depressives may also be distinguished from schizophrenics by slowness of reaction and by distant reactions.

It should be noted that few of these observations have been subjected to careful study. The claims require validation.

DEPRESSION RATING SCALES

A large number of depression rating scales, both self-rating scales and observer-rating scales, have been developed. Some of these have not been well validated and are seldom used. Others serve specialized functions. Several scales that have been well received and widely used are discussed in this section.

Observer-Rating

Hamilton Rating Scale for Depression (Hamilton, 1960). The Hamilton Depression Rating Scale was developed with patients "already diagnosed as suffering from affective disorder of depressive type." It consists of a 17-item list of symptoms to be marked for severity by a clinician on the basis of an interview. Equal weight is given by the rater to both intensity and frequency of symptoms. The primary purpose of the scale is to quantify the data obtained in an interview. Obviously, its value depends on

---

[1] "Close reaction proper—no significant departure from the stimulus word and relevant only if the stimulus is kept in mind (e.g., screen—'through'; breast—'two')." "Distant reaction—related to the stimulus word in a farfetched manner (e.g., masturbation—'loss'; party—'funeral'; breast—'frankness'; man—'creature'; boy friend—'strength')." "Blocking—offering no reaction word" (Rapaport et al., 1968).

the skill of the interviewer in obtaining and evaluating the necessary information. Among the 17 items listed in this scale are depressed mood, guilt, suicide, varieties of insomnia, retardation, hypochondriasis, and somatic symptoms. Some definitions of these items are provided; for example, depressed mood is defined as "gloomy attitude, pessimism about the future; feelings of sadness, a tendency to weep." It is rated on a 0 to 4 scale, where 0 represents the absence of this feature, 1 represents sadness, 2 represents occasional weeping, 3 represents frequent weeping, and 4 represents extreme symptoms. Likewise, guilt is rated on a 0 to 4 scale, the scores being determined by the presence of such features as self-reproach, ideas of guilt, concept of the illness as a punishment, delusions of guilt, and hallucinations.

The average interrater reliability for the scale from several studies was 0.875. No information about validity was provided by Hamilton. The scoring method may be either in terms of the sum of the rating obtained or expressed as factor scores on four factors derived from the scores from the first 49 male patients in Hamilton's original study.

Cutler and Kurland Depression Scale (Cutler and Kurland, 1961). The authors of the Cutler and Kurland Depression Scale claim that it can be used both by trained personnel and auxiliary staff who can be instructed in its use in 15 minutes. It consists of a checklist of 27 clearly defined items that are recorded simply as being present or absent. A good inter-rater reliability has been reported by the authors, but their claims for validity (especially specificity for depression) are limited.

Self-Rating-Scales

A number of self-rating scales devised for use with depressed patients are popular because of the ease of their administration. However, their limitations include the bias that results from self-assessment and their limited use with severely ill and semiliterate patients. For example, there is a tendency among patients with an hysterical personality to produce very high scores on self-rating scales. High scores indicate a severe illness. However, these patients are not regarded as severely depressed by clinical criteria, nor do they obtain high scores on observer-rated scales. Further, a number of very severely depressed patients with marked retardation are either incapable of completing these tests or complete them in an uncritical manner.

Beck Depression Inventory (Beck, 1967). The Depression Inventory consists of 21 sets of statements. Each set contains four or five sentences and the patient is asked to select the one statement that he feels is most applicable to him. For example, the patient would choose one of the following five sentences:

I do not feel sad.

I feel blue or sad.

I am blue or sad all the time and I cannot snap out of it.

I am so sad or unhappy that it is quite painful.

I am so sad or unhappy that I cannot stand it.

Beck advised that patients be assisted with the completion of this questionnaire by a person who reads through each group of statements with them. He reported detailed and relatively successful attempts to establish the reliability and validity of the depression inventory. The inventory has also been factor analyzed by several investigators, and has been used for the detection of depression in groups of unselected psychiatric patients and among medical inpatients.

Zung Self-Rating Depression Scale (SDS) (Zung, 1965). The Self-Rating Depression Scale consists of 20 items that patients score as "a little of the time," "some of the time," "part of the time," and "most of the time." The items include such statements as "I feel downhearted and blue," "I have trouble with constipation," "I get tired for no reason," "My life is pretty full." Zung has reported the use of this scale in a fairly large number of patients and claims that it is relatively insensitive to such factors as age, education, and social status. He also reports a significant correlation with MMPI *D* scale scores. Although there is a statistically significant difference in SDS scores for patients with a diagnosis of anxiety reaction, as compared with depressed patients, examination of the published data suggests that there may be considerable overlap. For example, the mean SDS score for outpatients with a diagnosis of depressive reaction was 64, whereas that for outpatients with a diagnosis of anxiety reaction was 54. Although this difference was statistically significant, there was a considerable overlap. Thus, although the scale may be useful in plotting the course of an illness, its usefulness for differentiating depression from anxiety is questionable.

CHAPTER ELEVEN

TREATMENT OF DEPRESSION

The selection of the most appropriate method of treatment for a depressed patient is based on the response to the following questions.

1. How serious is the risk of suicide?
2. Does the patient need hospitalization?
3. Does the patient require a somatic therapy (drugs and/or ECT) and/or psychotherapy?
4. Should the family be involved in the treatment process, and if so, to what extent?

Because depression is often a self-limiting illness, statistics on the success rates for various forms of treatment are often unreliable. In addition, depressed patients (as well as other groups of psychiatric and medical patients in general) often show a nonspecific placebo response that is not related to the characteristics—biochemical or psychological—of the particular therapy to which he has been exposed.

It has been widely demonstrated that the response to a particular treatment is to a considerable extent dependent on the patient's expectations. Thus, if he believes that he is receiving a potent therapy or drug, the probability of a good response is far greater than if he has doubts about the efficacy of the treatment. This applies both in circumstances when the patient is receiving a known treatment and when he is receiving an inactive compound (placebo). The response to the placebo is obviously rooted in the psychological response to the treatment situation.

There is difficulty in selecting the most appropriate treatment for the individual patient. Although we know that some depressed patients will respond well to electroconvulsive therapy and do poorly in psychotherapy, and that others will show no response or even retrogress if given electroconvulsive therapy and show a favorable response in psychotherapy, the decision as to which of these or other treatments the patient should be given is unfortunately often based on clinical impression instead of careful investigation (Mendels, 1967).

HOSPITALIZATION

The decision of whether to hospitalize a depressed patient hinges on several factors, including the suicidal risk, pathological interaction with family members, need for electroconvulsive therapy, and difficulties in establishing a therapeutic relationship. In general, there is a decreasing tendency to hospitalize psychiatric patients. To a large extent this is because people seek treatment early in the illness, and because drugs often can prevent significant deterioration.

Even if the illness is not very severe and if there is no significant risk of suicide, there may be an advantage to hospitalization if a pathologically ambivalent, hostile, or dependent relationship has been established between the depressive and his family. Such a relationship may contribute to the perpetuation of the illness, and removal from the environment is often beneficial. Furthermore, the controlled, protective environment of the hospital may itself contribute to the resolution of the illness. It is well known that many patients improve considerably simply as a result of admission to a hospital. This reduction in the severity of the illness may allow a therapeutic relationship to develop more easily than was previously possible.

PSYCHOTHERAPY

As we indicated in Chapter 5, there is disagreement about the nature of the psychodynamics of depressed patients, even among therapists who accept depression as basically a psychological disorder stemming from an inadequate resolution of conflicts experienced during crucial developmental stages. Those who conceive of depression as a primary biochemical abnormality or as genetically determined, often regard psychodynamics and psychotherapy as relatively unimportant except in supportive use. Behavior therapists who conceive of depression in terms of learning theory would base a psychotherapeutic approach on these principles.

Psychotherapy based on psychodynamic theory has the objective of re-

ANTIDEPRESSANT DRUGS / 103

solving a current episode and of bringing about an alteration in the underlying personality difficulties that provided a basis for the emergence of the illness; the basic general principles of psychotherapy apply to the treatment of depression. However, there are certain aspects of the psychotherapy of depressives that need to be highlighted.

1. *The depressive anticipates rejection.* It is therefore necessary for him to learn that the therapist accepts him. This acceptance must be seen as arising *in spite* of the patient's belief in his own unworthiness, and not *because* of it. The depressive may frequently perceive and interpret the therapist's behavior as rejecting; the therapist should avoid reacting to this with frustration or irritation. However, if a patient thinks that the therapist is accepting of him because of his self-punitive behavior, he may see this as confirmation of his poor self-concepts.

2. The therapist should avoid too rapid a release of the repressed anger and aggression, which might disrupt the therapeutic relationship or provide the necessary energy for a suicidal attempt.

3. Depressed patients frequently induce feelings of frustration and helplessness in therapists; every effort should be made by the therapist to recognize and handle these, lest he show his aggression.

4. The depressive should be provided with a certain amount of support and reassurance. Although it is necessary to avoid exaggerating this support and encouraging the development of undue dependency, an appropriate amount can be extremely beneficial. The therapist knows that depression is often self-limiting and that the patient's ideas and feelings are inappropriate and illogical. It may be of value if he is able to convey something of this. A number of clinicians have reported considerable relief on the part of depressives once they have recognized that although they feel desperate the condition will abate. Obviously this technique is more likely to be useful with people with mild to moderate forms of the illness than with those who are severely depressed.

ANTIDEPRESSANT DRUGS

In recent years a number of new drugs have been introduced for use with depressed patients. These antidepressant drugs have proved to be of considerable value. The drugs have probably resulted in a reduced use of electroconvulsive therapy, brought about improvement in patients who were chronically ill and resistant to other treatment, reduced the need for and duration of hospitalization, and made patients more responsive to psychotherapy.

TABLE 7: Antidepressant Drugs

Category	Generic Name	Trade Name
Tricyclic drugs (Imino-dibenzyl derivatives)	Imipramine	Tofranil
	Desmethyl-imipramine	Pertofrane Norpramine
	Amitriptyline	Elavil
	Nortriptyline	Aventyl
	Protriptyline	Vivactil
Monoamine oxidase (MAO) inhibitors	Isocarboxazid	Marplan
	Phenelzine	Nardil
	Nialamide	Niamid
	Tranylcypromine	Parnate
Direct stimulants	Amphetamine derivatives	Dexedrin
		Desoxyn, etc.

The antidepressant drugs can be placed in three broad groups according to their chemical structure and primary method of action. Of the three groups listed in Table 7, only two are of importance—the *tricyclics* and the *monoamine oxidase inhibitors* (MAOI). The third group—the direct stimulants—have little if any place in contemporary therapeutics. Although they are still widely used, there is little evidence that they are of value in the treatment of clinical depression, and they constitute a serious danger in that they are likely to give rise to habituation and addiction. The other two groups of drugs have chemical structures significantly different from one another, and appear to operate through different biochemical mechanisms; they do, however, have certain important effects in common. The effect on which most attention is currently focused is that they all increase the amount of biogenic amines available in the central nervous system (see page 77). The MAO inhibitors produce more serious complicating effects (especially occasional severe changes in blood pressure) than the tricyclics and are consequently not as widely used.

The combined use of antidepressant drugs in connection with either psychotherapy or electroconvulsive therapy is common. There is little evidence that the combination of drugs and ECT is of value. There is some evidence to support the combined use of drugs with psychotherapy for patients who are moderately or severely ill.

Recently some attention has been directed to the use of *phenothiazines* in the treatment of depression. The phenothiazines are a large group of drugs often referred to as major tranquilizers and used primarily in the treatment of schizophrenia. One phenothiazine (thioridazine or Mellaril) has been described as being of value in the treatment of patients with "agitated depression" or "anxiety plus depression." It has been suggested that there are grounds for separating these patients from other depressed patients.

Lithium carbonate has recently achieved considerable prominence in this area. It has been shown to be of value in the treatment of the acute manic episode, and there is some evidence that it is a valuable agent in the prevention of recurrent manic and depressive episodes (Schou 1968). Its use in the treatment of depression remains controversial but preliminary reports suggest that selected depressed patients may respond to it (Mendels et al., 1970).

ELECTROCONVULSIVE THERAPY

In 1938 Cerletti and Bini introduced electroconvulsive therapy (ECT). Several years later it became apparent that ECT, introduced for use in schizophrenia, was very effective in the treatment of depression. It soon became a bulwark of therapy for this condition. Indeed, until a few years ago, it was the most common method of treatment for hospitalized depressed patients.

The basic procedure of applying an electrode to each side of the forehead and passing a current of about 70 to 130 volts through the frontal lobes of the brain for a period of less than half a second still applies, but there have been certain significant modifications. Today most patients receive an intravenous barbiturate (such as Pentothal or Brevital) that rapidly induces anesthesia, together with an intravenous injection of a muscle relaxant (such as succinyl choline). The use of these or similar drugs has made the administration of ECT a much simpler procedure than in the past. The patient experiences little physical discomfort and the risk of complications is considerably reduced.

The number of treatments given and their frequency varies from patient to patient and indeed from hospital to hospital. In general there is little advantage, and perhaps considerable disadvantage, in administering too many treatments too frequently. The majority of depressed patients who respond to ECT do so after six to eight treatments given at the rate of three a week.

In spite of these significant changes in technique, our knowledge of this procedure has hardly advanced since its introduction. The gaps in our understanding are illustrated by the plethora of widely diverse and often contradictory theories that have sprung up around ECT. Such theories range from Ewall's postulate of "massage of the diencephalic centers" to Schilder's "victory over death with a joy of rebirth"; from Striess's suggestion that ECT results in a cerebral capillary spasm that eliminates diseased nerve cells to the statement by Glueck that "ECT is a highly condensed recapitulation of the process by means of which the fate of the egodystonic impulse is determined" (Kalinowsky and Hoch, 1961). Fear, hormones, amnesia, and "psychic shock" have all been invoked as the therapeutic modality. A considerable amount of theorizing has been based on the unsubstantiated hypothesis that depressed patients view ECT as a punitive procedure that provides absolution for their guilt feelings.

However, there is ample evidence that ECT does, in a significant number of patients, abort a depressive episode. The problem is to select those depressed patients who will show a favorable response to it. For a long time the general practice was to use ECT for patients diagnosed as suffering from manic-depressive illness or involutional depression. It was also used by some psychiatrists in the treatment of the more severe and refractory reactive depressive disorders. However, the realization that these diagnostic categories had significant limitations and the recent introduction of successful antidepressant drugs have highlighted the need for the development of a precise method of determining whether a particular depressed patient will respond to ECT or not.

Although the experimental evidence is relatively limited, it appears that a depressed patient whose clinical state is characterized by a history of previous favorable responses to ECT, early morning wakening, psychomotor retardation, and, to a lesser degree, a family history of depression, and by the absence of a history of neurotic traits in childhood, neurotic traits in adulthood, inadequate or maladjusted personality, hypochondriasis, and a hysterical attitude toward the current illness is likely to show a favorable response to ECT. To some extent this does, at least in part, parallel the dichotomy of endogenous and reactive depression (Mendels, 1965, 1967).

The most frequent and significant behavioral complications of ECT are loss of memory (both anterograde and retrograde), difficulty in concentration, and confusion. No other consistent psychological defect has been demonstrated in patients given ECT. It is possible that the recent introduction of unilateral ECT (here both electrodes are placed on *one* side of the head and the current is passed mainly through the nondominant cerebral hemisphere) may reduce the incidence and severity of these side effects. Preliminary evidence suggests that unilateral ECT may be as effective as bilateral ECT, with a lower complication rate because of the reduction in current passing through the dominant part of the brain. However, evidence is lacking as to whether the response is as lasting as that obtained from bilateral ECT.

The choice of a treatment program for each person must be based on the particular features present. It is necessary to individualize treatment instead of having a standard approach that is applied to every depressive.

AMERICAN PSYCHIATRIC ASSOCIATION'S OFFICIAL CLASSIFICATION OF THE AFFECTIVE DISORDERS

The Diagnostic and Statistical Manual for Mental Disorders, (APA, 1968) contains the American Psychiatric Association's latest classification of patients with a mood disturbance. This system is used by the American Psychological Association and other professional organizations.

In practice, problems and confusion frequently arise because of the multiple use of the term depression to describe a physiological mood state, a symptom, a syndrome and a disease entity. The difficulty is compounded by the often arbitrary use of a host of adjectives to delineate subtypes of depression. For example, a quick perusal of the literature will find such diagnostic categories as *psychotic* depression, *neurotic reactive* depression, *melancholia* (minor or major), *agitated* depression, *endogenous* depression, *schizo*-depression, depression with *chronic brain syndrome,* and *involutional* depression. Many of these approaches to the diagnosis of depression are based on dichotomies such as *retarded / agitated; psychotic / neurotic; endogenous / reactive; typical / atypical; autonomous / reactive.*

The APA diagnoses that include depression are:

A. **Major Affective Disorders** (also described as affective psychoses).

1. Manic-depressive illnesses (also described as manic-depressive psychoses).
   a. Manic type.
   b. Depressed type.
   c. Circular type.
   d. Other major affective disorders (also described as affective psychoses) including "mixed" manic-depressive illness.
2. Involutional melancholia.

B. **Psychotic Depressive Reaction.**

C. **Depressive Neurosis** (also described as reactive depression).

A. Major Affective Disorders

"This group of psychoses is characterized by a single disorder of mood, either extreme depression or elation, that dominates the mental life of the patient and is responsible for whatever loss of contact he has with his environment. The onset of the mood does not seem to be related directly to a precipitating life experience and therefore is distinguished from *Psychotic depressive reaction* and *Depressive neurosis.*"

"These disorders are marked by severe mood swings and a tendency to remission and recurrence. Patients may be given this diagnosis in the absence of a previous history of affective psychosis if there is no obvious precipitating event. This disorder is divided into three major subtypes: manic type, depressed type, and circular type."

1a. *Manic-depressive illness, manic type*

"This disorder consists exclusively of manic episodes. These episodes are characterized by excessive elation, irritability, talkativeness, flight of ideas, and accelerated speech and motor activity. Brief periods of depression sometimes occur, but they are never true depressive episodes."

1b. *Manic-depressive illness, depressed type* (Manic-depressive psychosis, depressed type)

"This disorder consists exclusively of depressive episodes. These episodes are characterized by severely depressed mood and by mental and motor retardation progressing occasionally to stupor. Uneasiness, apprehension, perplexity and agitation may also be present. When illusions, hallucinations, and delusions (usually of guilt or of hypochondriacal or paranoid ideas) occur, they are attributable to the dominant mood disorder. Because it is a primary mood disorder, this psychosis differs from the *Psychotic depressive reaction,* which is more easily attributable to precipitating stress."

1c. *Manic-depressive illness, circular type* (Manic-depressive psychosis, circular type)

"This disorder is distinguished by at least one attack of both a depressive episode and a manic episode. This phenomenon makes clear why manic and depressed types are combined into a single category."

1d. *Other major affective disorders* (Affective psychoses, other)

"Major affective disorders for which a more specific diagnosis has not been made are included here. It is also for 'mixed' manic-depressive illness, in which manic and depressive symptoms appear almost simultaneously. It does not include *Psychotic depressive reaction* or *Depressive neurosis*."

2. *Involutional Melancholia*

"This is a disorder occurring in the involutional period and characterized by worry, anxiety, agitation, and severe insomnia. Feelings of guilt and somatic preoccupations are frequently present and may be of delusional proportions. This disorder is distinguished from *Manic-depressive illness* by the absence of previous episodes; it is distinguished from *Schizophrenia* in that impaired reality testing is due to a disorder of mood; and it is distinguished from *Psychotic depressive reaction* in that the disorder of mood is not due to some experience. Opinion is divided as to whether this psychosis can be distinguished from the other affective disorders. It is, therefore, recommended that involutional patients not be given this diagnosis unless all other affective disorders have been ruled out."

B. Psychotic Depressive Reaction
(Reactive Depressive Psychosis)

"This psychosis is distinguished by a depressive mood attributable to some experience. Ordinarily the individual has no history of repeated depressions or cyclothymic mood swings. The differentiation between this condition and *Depressive neurosis* depends on whether the reaction impairs reality testing or functional adequacy enough to be considered a psychosis."

C. Depressive Neurosis

"This disorder is manifested by an excessive reaction of depression due to an internal conflict or to an identifiable event such as the loss of a love object or cherished possession. It is to be distinguished from *Involutional melancholia* and *Manic-depressive illness*. *Reactive depressions* or *depressive reactions* are to be classified here."

BIBLIOGRAPHY

Abraham, K. Notes on the psychoanalytic investigation and treatment of manic-depressive insanity and allied conditions (1911). In *Selected papers on psychoanalysis*. New York: Basic Books, 1960. Pp. 137–156.

American Psychiatric Association. *Diagnostic and statistical manual of mental disorders*. (2nd ed.) Washington: APA, 1968.

Arieti, S. Manic-depressive psychosis. In S. Arieti (Ed.), *American handbook of psychiatry*. Vol. 1. New York: Basic Books, 1959.

Assael, M. and Thein, M. Blood acetaldehyde levels in affective disorders. *The Israel Annals of Psychiatry and Related Disciplines*, 1964, **2**, 228–234.

Balint, M. New beginning and the paranoid and the depressive syndromes. *International Journal of Psychoanalysis*, 1952, **33**, 214–224.

Bandrup, E. and Bandrup, A. A controlled investigation of plasma lipids in manic depressives. *British Journal of Psychiatry*, 1967, **113**, 987–992.

Batchelor, I.R.C. Suicide in old age. In E.S. Schneidman and N.L. Farberow (Eds.), *Clues to suicide*. New York: McGraw Hill Co., 1957.

Beck, A.T. *Depression: Clinical, experimental, and theoretical aspects*. New York: Harper & Row, 1967.

Becker, J. Achievement-related characteristics of manic-depressives. *Journal of Abnormal Social Psychology*, 1960, **60**, 334–339.

Becker, J., Spielberger, C.D., and Parker, J.B. Value achievement and authoritarian attitudes in psychiatric patients. *Journal of Clinical Psychology*, 1963, **19**, 57–61.

Benedek, T. Toward the biology of the depressive constellation. *Journal of the American Psychoanalytical Association*, 1965, **4**, 389.

Bibring, E. The mechanism of depression, in P. Greenacre (Ed.), *Affective disorders*. New York: International Universities Press, Inc., 1965. Pp. 13–48.

113

Bliss, E.L., Wilson, V.B., and Zwanziger, J. Changes in brain norepinephrine in self-stimulating and "aversive" animals. *Journal of Psychiatric Research,* 1966, **4,** 59–63.

Bonime, W. The psychodynamics of neurotic depression. In S. Arieti (Ed.), *American handbook of psychiatry.* Vol. III. New York: Basic Books, Inc., 1966.

Bunney, W.E., Jr., Mason, J.W., and Hamburg, D.A. Correlations between behavioral variables and urinary 17-hydroxycorticosteroids in depressed patients. *Psychosomatic Medicine,* 1965, **27,** 299–308.

Busfield, B.L., Wechsler, H., and Barnum, W.J. Studies of salivation in depression. *Archives of General Psychiatry,* 1961, **51,** 472–477.

Cade, J.F.J. A significant elevation of plasma magnesium levels in schizophrenia and depressive states. *Medical Journal of Australia,* 1964, **1,** 195–196.

Campbell, J.D. *Manic-depressive disease.* Philadelphia: J.B. Lippincott Co., 1953.

Carney, M.W.P., Roth, M., and Garside, R.F. The diagnosis of depressive syndromes and the prediction of ECT response. *British Journal of Psychiatry,* 1965, **3,** 659–674.

Clayton, P.J., Pitts, F.N., and Winokur, G. Affective disorder IV. Mania. *Psychiatry,* 1965, **6,** 313.

Cohen, M.B., Baker, G., Cohen, R., Fromm-Reichmann, F., and Weigert, E. An intensive study of twelve cases of manic-depressive psychosis. *Psychiatry,* 1954, **17,** 103–137.

Colbert, J. and Harrow, M. Psychomotor retardation in depressive syndromes. *Journal of Nervous and Mental Diseases,* 1967, **145,** 405–419.

Collomb, H. Methodological problems in cross-cultural research. *International Journal of Psychiatry,* 1967, **3,** 17–19.

Coppen, A. The biochemistry of affective disorders. *British Journal of Psychiatry,* 1967, **113,** 1237–1264.

Cutler, R.P. and Kurland, H.D. Clinical quantification of depressive reactions. *Archives of General Psychiatry,* 1961, **5,** 280–285.

Dahlstrom, W.G., and Welsh, G.S. *An MMPI handbook.* Minneapolis: University of Minnesota Press, 1962.

Dement, W., and Kleitman, H. Cyclic variations in EEG during sleep and their relation to eye movements, body motility, and dreaming. *Electroencephalography and Clinical Neurophysiology,* 1957, **9,** 673–690.

Denber, N.C.B. Electroencephalographic findings during chlorpromazine—diethazine treatment. *Journal of Nervous and Mental Diseases,* 1958, **126,** 392–398.

Dowling, R.H., and Knox, S.J. Somatic symptoms in depressive illness. *British Journal of Psychiatry,* 1964, **110,** 720–722.

Durkheim, E. *Le suicide; etude de sociology.* Translated by J.A. Spaulding and G. Simpson. Glencoe, Ill.: Free Press, 1951.

Eaton, J.W., and Weil, R.J. *Culture and mental disorders.* Glencoe, Ill.: Free Press, 1955.

Elsasser, G. Ovarial function and body constitution in female inmates of mental hospitals; special reference to schizophrenia. *Archives of Psychiatry* (Berlin), 1952, **188,** 218.

Engel, G.L. *Psychological development in health and disease.* Philadelphia: Saunders, 1962.

Farberow, N.L., and Schneidman, E.S. *The cry for help.* New York: McGraw Hill, 1965.

Field, M.J. *Journal of Mental Science,* 1958, **104**, 1043–1051.

Flach, F.F. *Proceedings of the IVth world congress of psychiatry, Madrid, Spain.* Exerpta Medica International Congress Series No. 150 Amsterdam: Exerpta Medica Foundation, 1966.

Freud, S. Mourning and melancholia (1917). Reprinted in *Collected papers,* Vol. 4. London: Hogarth Press and the Institute of Psychoanalysis, 1950. Pp. 152–172.

Funkenstein, D.H., Greenblatt, M., and Solomon, H.C. An autonomic nervous system test of prognostic significance in relation to electroshock treatment. *Psychosomatic Medicine,* 1952, **14,** 347.

Gershon, E.S., Cromer, M., and Klerman, G.L. Hostility and depression. *Psychiatry,* 1968, **31,** 224–235.

Gibson, R.W. *Comparison of the family background and early life experience of the manic-depressive and schizophrenic patient.* Final Report of Office of Naval Research Contract [Nonr-751 (00)]. Washington, D.C.: Washington School of Psychiatry, 1957.

Gillespie, R.D. The clinical differentiation of types of depression. *Guys Hospital Reports,* 1929, **79,** 306–344.

Glassman, A. H. Indoleamines and affective disorders. Psychosomatic Medicine **2,** 107–114, 1969.

Goldstein, I.G. The relationship of muscle tension and autonomic activity to psychiatric disorders. *Psychosomatic Medicine,* 1965, **27,** 39–52.

Grewel, F. Psychiatric differences in Ashkenazim and Sephardim. *Psychiatria, Neurologea, Neurochirurgia,* 1967, **70,** 339–347.

Grinker, R.R., Sr., Miller, J., Sabshin, M., Nann, R., and Nunnally, J.C. *The phenomena of depressions.* New York: Paul B. Hoeber, Inc., 1961.

Gutheil, E.A. Reactive depressions. In S. Arieti (Ed.), *American handbook of psychiatry.* Vol. 1. New York: Basic Books, 1959. Pp. 345–352.

Hamilton, M., and White, J.M. Clinical syndromes in depressive states. *Journal of Mental Science,* 1959, **105,** 985–998.

Hamilton, M. A rating scale for depression. *Journal of Neurology, Neurosurgery and Psychiatry,* 1960, **23,** 56–62.

Harris, R.E., and Lingoes, J.C. *Subscales for the MMPI: An aid to profile interpretation.* Mimeographed. San Francisco: Department of Psychiatry, University of California, 1955.

Hendin, H. Black suicide. *Archives of General Psychiatry,* 1969, **21,** 407–422.

Hordern, A. *Depressive states, a pharmacotherapeutic study.* Springfield: Thomas, 1965.

Kalinowsky, and L.B., and Hoch, P.H. *Somatic treatments in psychiatry.* New York: Grune and Stratton, 1961.

Kallman, F. Genetic aspects of psychoses. In *Biology of mental health and disease,* (Milbank Memorial Fund) New York: Hoeber. Pp. 283–302.

Kaufman, I.C., and Rosenblum, L.A. The reaction to separation in infant monekeys: Anaclytic depression and conservation withdrawal. *Psychosomatic Medicine,* 1967, **29,** 648–675.

Kendell, R.E. Relationship between aggression and depression. *Archives of General Psychiatry,* 1970, **22,** 308.

Kiloh, L.G., and Garside, R.F. The independence of neurotic depression and endogenous depression. *British Journal of Psychiatry,* 1963, **109,** 451–463.

Klein, M. Contributions to the psycho-genesis of the manic-depressive states. In *Contributions to psychoanalysis,* 1921–1945. London: Hogarth Press, 1948.

Kraepelin, E. *Lectures on clinical psychiatry.* New York: Hafner Publishing Co., 1913. (Reprinted 1968 by Hafner.)

Kraines, S.H. Manic-depressive syndrome: A physiologic disease. *Diseases of the Nervous System,* 1966, **27,** 3–19.

Lange, J. *Handbuch der Geisteskrankheiten.* Vol 2. Berlin: Springer, 1928.

Laughlin, H. P. *The neuroses in clinical practice.* Philadelphia: W. B. Saunders Co., 1956.

Leighton, A. H., et al. *Psychiatric disorders among the Yoruba.* Ithaca: Cornell University Press, 1963.

Lesse, S. The multivariant masks of depression. *American Journal of Psychiatry,* 1968, **124,** (May Supplement), 35–40.

Lin, T. Y. *Psychiatry,* 1953, **16,** 313.

Lorenz, M. Language behavior in manic patients. An equalitative study. *Archives of Neurology and Psychiatry,* 1953, **69,** 14.

McGough, W. E., Williams, E., and Blackley, J. Changing patterns of psychiatric illness among Negroes of the southeastern United States. Proceedings of the IVth World Congress of Psychiatry. Madrid, Spain, *Excerpta Medica International Congress Series No. 150* Amsterdam, Excerpta Medica Foundation, 1966.

McC. Anderson, W., and Dawson, J. The clinical manifestations of depressive illness with abnormal Acetyl Methyl Carbinol metabolism. *Journal of Mental Science,* 1962, **108,** 80–87.

Mendels, J. The prediction of response to electroconvulsive therapy. *American Journal of Psychiatry,* 1967, **124,** 153–159.

Mendels, J., and Cochrane, C. The nosology of depression: The endogenous-reactive concept. *American Journal of Psychiatry,* 1968, **124,** (May Supplement) 1–11.

Mendels, J. Urinary 17-Ketosteroid fractionation in depression: A preliminary report. *British Journal of Psychiatry,* 1969, **115,** 581–585.

Mendels, J., and Hawkins, D. R. Sleep studies in depression. In *Proceedings of the symposium on recent advances in the psychobiology of affective disorders.* Bethesda, Md.: National Institute of Mental Health, 1970.

Mendels, J., and Cochrane, C. Syndromes of depression and the response to E.C.T. In Preparation, 1970.

Mendels, J., Secunda, S., and Dyson, W. A Double-blind controlled trial of lithium in the treatment of depression. In Preparation, 1970.

Mendelson, M. *Psychoanalytic concepts of depression.* Springfield: Thomas, 1960.

Menninger, K., Mayman, M., and Pruyser, P. *The vital balance.* New York, Viking Press, 1963.

O'Connor, J. P., Stefic, E. C., and Gresock, C. J. Some patterns of depression. *Journal of Clinical Psychology*, 1957, **13**, 122–125.

Palmai, G., Blackwell, B., Maxwell, A.E., Morgenstern, F. Patterns of salivary flow in depressive illness and during treatment. *British Journal of Psychiatry*, 1967, **113**, 1297–1308.

Paulson, G. W., and Gottlieb, G. A longitudinal study of the electroencephalographic arousal response in depressed patients. *Journal of Nervous and Mental Diseases*, 1961, **133**, 524–528.

Perris, C. A study of bipolar (manic-depressive) and unipolar recurrent depressive psychoses. *Acta Psychiatrica Scandinavia*, 1966, **42**, Supplement 194.

Pokorny, A. D. Suicide rates in various psychiatric disorders. *Journal of Nervous and Mental Diseases*, 1964, **139**, 499–506.

Pollitt, J. *Depression and its treatment.* Springfield: Chas. C. Thomas, 1965.

Rapaport, D., Gill, M. M., and Schafer, R. *Diagnostic psychological testing.* R. R. Holt (Ed.). New York: International Universities Press, 1968.

Redlich, F. C., and Freedman, D. X. *The theory and practice of psychiatry.* New York: Basic Books, Inc., 1966.

Reisman, D., Glazer, N., and Denney, R., *The lonely crowd.* New York: Doubleday Anchor Books, 1953.

Rimon, R., Steinback, A., and Huhmar, E. Electromyographic findings in depressive patients. *Journal of Psychosomatic Research*, 1966, **10**, 159–170.

Robins, E., et al. The communication of suicidal intent: A study of 134 consecutive cases of successful (completed) suicide. *American Journal of Psychiatry*, 1959, **115**, 724–733.

Rosen, A. *Development of some new MMPI scales for differentiation of psychiatric syndromes within an abnormal population.* (Ph.D. Dissertation, University of Minnesota.) Cited in Dahlstrom and Walsh, 1962.

Rosenthal, S. H., and Klerman, G. L. Content and consistency in the endogenous depressive pattern. *British Journal of Psychiatry*, 1966, **112**, 471–484.

Rosenthal, S. H., and Gudeman, J. E. The endogenous depressive pattern: An empirical investigation. *Archives of General Psychiatry*, 1967, **16**, 241–249.

Rubin, R. T., and Mandell, A. J. Adrenal cortical activity in pathological emotional states: A review. *American Journal of Psychiatry*, 1966, **123**, 387–400.

Sachar, E. J. Corticosteroid responses to psychotherapy of depressions. *Archives of General Psychiatry*, 1967, **16**, 461–470.

Sainsbury, P. Suicide and depression. In A. Coppen and A. Walk (Eds.), *Recent developments in affective disorders.* Special Publication #2. London: Royal Medico-Psychological Association, 1968.

Sainz, A., and Bigelow, N. Relative antidepressant activity of various chemical groups. *Third world congress of psychiatry.* Vol. III. Montreal: McGill University Press, 1961. Pp. 1387–1393.

Schachter, S. The interaction of cognitive and physiological determinants of emotional state. In P. H. Leiderman and D. Shapiro (Eds.), *Psychological approaches to social behavior.* Stanford, Calif.: Stanford University Press, 1964.

Schildkraut, J. J. The catecholamine hypothesis of affective disorders: A review of supporting evidence. *American Journal of Psychiatry*, 1965, **122**, 509–522.

Schmale, A. H., Jr. Relationship of separation and depression to disease. I. A report on a hospitalized medical population. *Psychosomatic Medicine*, 1958, **20**, 259–277.

Schneider, K. Die Schichtung Des Emotionale, Lebens Und Der Aufbau Der Depressianzustande. *Z. Ges. Neurologie Psychiatrie*, 1920, **58**, 281.

Schou, M. Lithium in psychiatric therapy and prophylaxis. *Journal of Psychiatric Research*, 1968, **6**, 67–95.

Schwab, J. J., Bialow, F., Holzer, C. E., Brown, J. M., and Stevenson, B. E. Sociocultural aspects of depression in medical inpatients. *Archives of General Psychiatry*, 1967, **17**, 533–538.

Shagass, C., and Schwartz, M. Cerebral cortical reactivity in psychotic depressions. *Archives of General Psychiatry*, 1962, **6**, 235–242.

Shaw, D. M. Mineral metabolism, mania, and melancholia. *British Medical Journal*, 1966, **2**, 262–267.

Shields, J. *Monozygotic twins*. New York: Oxford University Press, 1962.

Slater, E. Psychiatric and neurotic illnesses in twins. In *Medical Research Council Special Report Series, No. 278*. London: Her Majesty's Stationery Office, 1953.

Spitz, R. A. Anaclitic Depression. In A. Freud et al. (Eds.), *The Psychoanalytic Study of the Child*. Vol 2. New York: International Universities Press, 1946.

Stenstedt, A. A study in manic-depressive psychosis: Clinical, social, and genetic investigations. *Acta Psychiatrica Scandinavia*, 1952, Suppl. 79.

Stenstedt, A. Involutional melancholia: An etiologic, clinical and social study of endogenous depression in later life, with special reference to genetic factors. *Acta Psychiatrica Scandinavia*, 1959, Suppl. 127.

Thorpe, J. G. The current status of prognostic test indicators for electroconvulsive therapy. *Psychosomatic Medicine*, 1962, **24**, 554–568.

Van Praag, H. M., Uleman, A. M., and Spitz, J. C. The vital syndrome interview. *Psychiatrie Neurologie Neurochirgarie*, 1965, **68**, 329–346.

Van Praag, H. M., and Leisnse, B. Depression, glucose tolerance, peripheral glucose uptake and their alterations under the influence of anti-depressive drugs of the hydrazine type. *Psychopharmacologia*, 1965, **8**, 67–78.

Vitols, M. M., and Prange, A. J. Cultural aspects of the relatively low incidence of depression in southern Negroes. *International Journal of Social Psychiatry*, 1962, **8**, 104–112.

Whatmore, G. B., and Ellis, R. M., Jr. Further neurophysiologic aspects of depressed states: An electromyographic study. *Archives of General Psychiatry*, 1962, **6**, 243–253.

Wheat, W. D. Motivational aspects of suicide in patients during and after psychiatric treatment. *Southern Medical Journal*, 1960, **53**, 273.

Whybrow, P. C., and Mendels, J. Toward a biology of depression: Some suggestions from neurophysiology. *American Journal of Psychiatry*, 1969, **125**, 1491–1500.

Winokur, G. Genetic principles in the clarification of clinical issues in affective disorders. In A. J. Mandell and M. P. Mandell (Eds.), *Psychochemical research in man*. New York: Academic Press, 1969.

Yap, P. M. *Suicide in Hong Kong*. London: Oxford University Press, 1958.

Yap, P. M. Phenomenology of affective disorder in Chinese and other cultures. In

A. V. S. DeReuck and R. Porter (Eds.), *Transcultural psychiatry*. A Ciba Foundation Symposium, Boston: Little, Brown & Co., 1965.

Zung, W. W. K. A self-rating depression scale. *Archives of General Psychiatry*, 1965, **12,** 63–70.

INDEX